JUL 14 2014

SPOTLIGHT

DETROIT & ANN ARBOR

LAURA MARTONE

Contents

DETROIT AND SOUTHEAST MICHIGAN

Although Detroit's official motto—*Speramus meliora; resurget cineribus*—resulted from a catastrophic fire that nearly destroyed the fledgling town in 1805, its meaning could just as easily refer to modern times: "We hope for better things. It will rise from the ashes." This is a city, after all, that has witnessed its share of soaring highs and crushing lows, and yet has always managed to come back swinging.

Detroit truly hit the map when Henry Ford's assembly line transformed the town—and the world—forever. With the assistance of the "Big Three" (Ford, General Motors, and Chrysler), the Motor City thrived during the first half of the 20th century. Reliance on a single industry, however, inevitably led to downswings that mimicked those of the auto industry, plunging the racially divided metropolis into years of crime and unemployment—modern problems that have, at times, been exaggerated by the national media.

But the Motor City is defined less by its adversity and more by its innovation and fortitude. Crime is not the crippling issue it once was, and development has helped to revitalize the downtown area. Unofficially nicknamed the Renaissance City in the 1970s, Detroit has finally begun to shed its troubled past. Although it's still a work-in-progress, this tenacious town—also known for its Motown music, rock 'n' roll vibe, and legendary sports figures—has improved its tarnished image since the turn of the new millennium, and nowhere is that more apparent than along the waterfront.

Dominating the Detroit skyline, the

HIGHLIGHTS

LOOK FOR **◖** TO FIND RECOMMENDED SIGHTS, ACTIVITIES, DINING, AND LODGING.

◖ GM Renaissance Center: Towering above the Detroit River since the late 1970s, the 73-story Ren Cen is home to GM's world headquarters, a 1,300-room hotel, a fitness center, a movie theater, and numerous shops and restaurants. Visitors can take a free, one-hour tour of the enormous complex, which also includes a vintage auto collection, a tropical atrium overlooking the river, and incredible views of the Detroit and Windsor skylines (page 12).

◖ Belle Isle State Park: Situated in the Detroit River, Belle Isle has long been a treasured spot for visitors and area residents alike. Highlights include designated biking paths, a zoo, a swimming beach, a conservatory, golf facilities, the Dossin Great Lakes Museum, two fishing piers, and numerous historic edifices (page 13).

◖ Greektown: One of several ethnic enclaves in the Detroit metropolitan area, this historic neighborhood invites visitors to experience Greek culture at its best. Here, you'll find the longstanding Pegasus Taverna, the annual Detroit Greek Independence Day Parade, and a flashy casino (page 18).

◖ The Cultural Center: Art and culture lovers flock to this part of Midtown, which boasts two art museums, three history museums, a science center, an anthropology museum, a children's museum, and several well-preserved Victorian structures, plus nearby theaters and art galleries (page 18).

◖ Hamtramck: Founded in the early 20th century, this village has long lured Polish immigrants and other Europeans. While the neighborhood is more culturally diverse these days, visitors can still come here for Polish sausages, European baked goods, and traditional artwork (page 37).

◖ The Henry Ford: At this curious complex, visitors can view Henry Ford's childhood home, Thomas Edison's Menlo Park laboratory, President Kennedy's limousine, Rosa Parks's bus, and a working 19th-century farm. You can also hitch a ride to the Ford truck assembly plant for an informative walking tour (page 39).

◖ Lake Erie Metropark: South of Detroit lies this well-preserved, 1,607-acre recreation area, popular among hikers, bird-watchers, anglers, golfers, cross-country skiers, and those who appreciate stunning views of the Detroit River, Lake Erie, and North America's first international wildlife refuge (page 48).

◖ Woodward Dream Cruise: This annual mid-August parade down Woodward Avenue, from Ferndale to Pontiac, has become the world's largest one-day automotive event, luring 1.5 million people and more than 40,000 classic cars from around the globe (page 50).

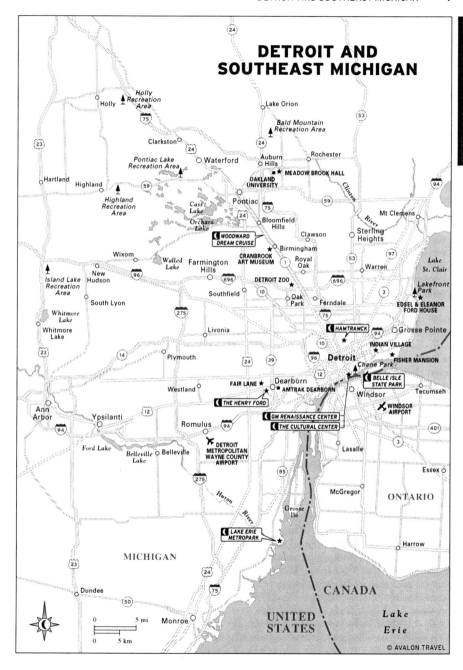

DETROIT AND SOUTHEAST MICHIGAN

Holly
Holly Recreation Area
Lake Orion
Bald Mountain Recreation Area
Clarkston
Auburn Hills
Rochester
Waterford
MEADOW BROOK HALL
Hartland
Highland
Pontiac Lake Recreation Area
OAKLAND UNIVERSITY
Highland Recreation Area
Cass Lake
Pontiac
Orchard Lake
Bloomfield Hills
WOODWARD DREAM CRUISE
Clawson
Mt Clemens
Sterling Heights
Wixom
Walled Lake
Farmington Hills
Birmingham
CRANBROOK ART MUSEUM
Royal Oak
Warren
Lake St. Clair
New Hudson
Island Lake Recreation Area
DETROIT ZOO
Lakefront Park
South Lyon
Southfield
Oak Park
Ferndale
EDSEL & ELEANOR FORD HOUSE
Whitmore Lake
Whitmore Lake
Livonia
HAMTRAMCK
Grosse Pointe
INDIAN VILLAGE
Plymouth
Detroit
FISHER MANSION
Chene Park
BELLE ISLE STATE PARK
Westland
Dearborn
FAIR LANE
AMTRAK DEARBORN
Windsor
Tecumseh
THE HENRY FORD
WINDSOR AIRPORT
Ann Arbor
Ypsilanti
Romulus
GM RENAISSANCE CENTER
THE CULTURAL CENTER
Lasalle
Ford Lake
DETROIT METROPOLITAN WAYNE COUNTY AIRPORT
Belleville Lake
Belleville
Essex
McGregor
ONTARIO
Grosse Ile
LAKE ERIE METROPARK
Harrow
MICHIGAN
Dundee
CANADA
Monroe
UNITED STATES
Lake Erie

0   5 mi
0   5 km

© AVALON TRAVEL

once-controversial Renaissance Center has undergone an extensive renovation, transforming the distinctive office, hotel, and retail complex into the world headquarters of General Motors. In addition, the city has embarked upon an ambitious development project along the Detroit River, which it shares with Windsor, Canada. When completed, the Detroit Riverfront will comprise a new harbor, the expanded William G. Milliken State Park, and a network of biking and jogging trails. Other recent downtown enhancements include a new ballpark for the Detroit Tigers, an adjacent football stadium for the Detroit Lions, and three casino resorts.

Detroit's many suburbs have also experienced a revival, marked by the opening of such attractions as the Holocaust Memorial Center in Farmington Hills and the Arab American National Museum in Dearborn, both of which celebrate the rich diversity of Detroit's people. Beyond the greater Detroit metropolitan area, visitors will discover a wealth of activities in Southeast Michigan, from skiing on Mt. Holly to watching the Woodward Dream Cruise. Despite decades of struggle, it seems that Detroit and its surrounding towns are finally on the upswing, once again affirming the city's two-century-old motto.

ORIENTATION

Almost prophetically, early Detroit was laid out like the spokes of a wheel. The plan— laid down by Judge Augustus Woodward, the first chief justice of the new Michigan territory—foreshadowed the city's major industry by more than a century. Woodward arrived in 1805 to find no more than a burned-out trading post on the narrow straits of the river—*détroit,* incidentally, means "straits." While little else remains of Woodward's grandiose plans to make Detroit the "Paris of the Midwest," the city's main streets—Jefferson Avenue, Gratiot Avenue, Woodward Avenue, Grand River Avenue, Michigan Avenue, and Fort Street— still echo that early hexagonal grid, shooting off at diagonal angles from a central axis. Woodward serves as the city's main dividing

line, splitting the landmass and its residents into east and west.

Compared to most U.S. urban areas, Detroit isn't too difficult to navigate. Though the city, its suburbs, and the rest of Southeast Michigan constitute a sprawling tapestry of distinct neighborhoods and communities, several bisecting highways and interstates make it easy to get around. For instance, I-75 snakes through downtown Detroit, linking southern towns like Monroe to northern destinations like Royal Oak, Pontiac, and Holly. Other major routes include I-96 from Lansing; I-696, which passes through Farmington Hills, Southfield, and Ferndale; and I-94, which cuts across the southern part of the Heartland, passes north of Detroit's Cultural Center and west of the Grosse Pointe suburbs, and heads north toward Port Huron.

PLANNING YOUR TIME

Southeast Michigan is a relatively small area, easy to traverse with a car. Several major routes link Detroit and its suburbs to other parts of the state, including I-75 from Flint, I-96 from Lansing, or I-94 from Battle Creek. Getting here via other forms of transportation is also a snap. The Detroit Metro Airport (DTW) serves as a hub for Delta Air Lines. In addition, Amtrak serves Dearborn, Detroit, Royal Oak, Birmingham, and Pontiac. Greyhound also offers regular bus services to three stations in the area: Detroit, Southfield, and Pontiac.

Unlike other parts of Michigan, Detroit and its suburbs aren't terribly dependent on the shifting seasons. Most museums, shops, and restaurants are open in winter as well as summer. No matter when you visit, however, you'll need at least three days to explore the region's key attractions, such as downtown Detroit and the Henry Ford complex in Dearborn. Five days is preferable, especially if you plan to make a trip across the border to Windsor, Ontario, in Canada.

Just remember that Detroit is a big, unpredictable city, and crime can definitely be a concern here. Tourist areas, such as the waterfront and the Cultural Center, are well patrolled, but it's important to stay vigilant even in relatively safe areas. For added protection, always travel with someone else, hide your money and identification beneath your clothing, and leave valuable jewelry back at home. It's also helpful to know the location of a few different police stations, just in case.

For more information about Detroit and its suburbs, consult the **Detroit Metro Convention & Visitors Bureau** (211 W. Fort St., Ste. 1000, Detroit, 313/202-1800, www.visitdetroit.com, 9am-5pm Mon.-Fri.) or **Travel Michigan** (Michigan Economic Development Corporation, 300 N. Washington Sq., Lansing, 888/784-7328, www.michigan.org).

HISTORY

Few think of Detroit as an old city. But it is, in fact, one of the Midwest's oldest, founded in 1701 by Antoine de la Mothe Cadillac (born Antoine Laumet) for King Louis XIV of France.

Early Detroit was alternately ruled by the British and the French. In 1763, Pontiac, the Ottawa war chief, ordered an attack on British posts all over Michigan. Tired of the abuse suffered by the British army, Pontiac united the many Indian nations living around Detroit in a determined effort to capture the fort and restore French rule. Chiefs of the Ottawa, Huron, Potawatomi, and Chippewa tribes attended a secret war council. According to legend, however, a squaw tipped off the British, and Pontiac's men were met by a waiting British army. Rebuffed and defeated, Pontiac was later assassinated in 1769. Today, Pontiac's Rebellion is still regarded as one of the most formidable Native American uprisings in American history.

In 1783, Britain yielded the area to the United States in the Treaty of Paris. Local tribes, however, disputed the U.S. claim, so it wasn't until 1796 that Detroit finally unfurled the stars and stripes. The city fell again during the War of 1812 but was recaptured by the Americans a year later. Despite discouraging reports from initial settlers, people continued to pour in from the east. Between 1830 and 1860,

the population doubled with every decade, and the city became best known as a nucleus of beer brewing and stove making.

By the turn of the 20th century, the auto industry had changed everything, making Detroit the fifth-largest U.S. city. The state's first self-propelled vehicle was likely a steam-powered car built by John and Thomas Clegg of Memphis, Michigan, in 1884. Later, Ransom Olds of Lansing developed a gasoline-powered auto and founded the Olds Motor Vehicle Company. In 1896, Charles C. King, an engineer and auto designer, drove the first car through the streets of Detroit; in the same year, Henry Ford tested his Quadricycle, which chugged along fairly well, despite no brakes and no reverse gear.

It was Ford and his later perfection of the assembly line that changed the face of the city—and America—seemingly overnight. Between 1905 and 1924, thousands of immigrants poured in from all over the world, attracted by Henry Ford's then-unheard-of wage of $5 per day. By 1917, 23 companies in Detroit and its suburbs were busy assembling vehicles for an ever-eager public. The Motor City had arrived.

By the 1930s and 1940s, Detroit was the place to be. Lively and full of energy, it was home to after-hours bars known as "blind pigs" (that is, police—"pigs"—turned a "blind eye" to Prohibition-era hideouts that served liquor) and "black and tan" clubs where people of all races mingled. But things began to sour after World War II. As in other U.S. cities, the middle class began to head for the suburbs. Bigger and better freeways took people farther and farther away from the heart of the city, leaving behind vacant storefronts, vacant houses, empty streets, and empty lives too soon filled by poverty and crime.

The 1960s were difficult years. One bright spot was the birth of the Motown Sound, which began in the tiny basement studio of Berry Gordy Jr. Like the city, Motown had a hard-driving beat, and it quickly took over airwaves across the country. Detroit became known for producing more than cars, with

HAUNTED DETROIT

America's major cities all have their share of tragic histories, ranging from notorious murders to massive flu epidemics to calamitous fires. Such incidents have often inspired the belief that some buildings, cemeteries, and other historic places are haunted by the spirits of long-ago victims. Detroit is no exception. Founded well over three centuries ago, the Motor City has certainly witnessed a plethora of terrible incidents, from violent crimes to deadly race riots, so it may come as no surprise that it, too, has its share of haunted locales. If you enjoy visiting such places, here are nine of the most popular in and around the city:

- **Fair Lane:** Completed in 1914, Henry Ford's grand estate Fair Lane (1 Fair Lane Dr., Dearborn, 313/884-4222, www.henryfordestate. org) encompasses more than 1,300 acres, at the center of which lies an impressive mansion that served as the home of Henry and Clara Ford from 1915 until 1950. Although most visitors come to stroll amid the well-landscaped grounds and tour the well-appointed rooms of the main house, others are hoping to catch a glimpse of the former butler, whose spirit supposedly continues to clean, fix, and straighten the rooms as he once did in life.

- **Fort Shelby Hotel:** In 1927, famed architect Albert Kahn erected a 21-story tower beside the 10-story structure that had been built on the corner of Lafayette Boulevard and 1st Street in 1916. Together, the two buildings comprised the Fort Shelby Hotel,

whose fortunes rose and fell with those of Detroit. Following an extensive renovation mid-2007-late 2008, the buildings reopened as a DoubleTree Suites by Hilton Hotel (525 W. Lafayette Blvd., 313/963-5600, http://doubletree3.hilton.com) and the Fort Shelby Tower Apartments (527 W. Lafayette Blvd., 313/962-1010, www.fortshelby.com), but no matter how fancy it might look these days, the former Fort Shelby Hotel hasn't quite escaped its rocky history. Some visitors, after all, still claim to have seen the loitering ghost of a drunken homeless man who allegedly drowned in the once-flooded basement.

- **Historic Elmwood Cemetery:** Established in 1846, the 86-acre Historic Elmwood Cemetery (1200 Elmwood Ave., 313/567-3453, www.elmwoodhistoriccemetery.org) is the oldest continuously operating, nondenominational cemetery in Michigan. It's also the site of the Battle of Bloody Run, an ambush by Chief Pontiac's army on British soldiers, supposedly making it one of the city's best ghost-hunting locations.

- **Historic Fort Wayne:** While Historic Fort Wayne (6325 W. Jefferson Ave., 313/833-1805 or 810/853-8573, www.hauntedfortwaynedetroit.com), which was constructed in 1845 on the banks of the Detroit River, never actually endured a battle, the crumbling structure certainly still has a curious history. After all, it served as a major staging area for American soldiers during the Civil War and both World Wars, and it also housed

---

"Hitsville U.S.A." churning out rhythmic top-10 tunes by artists such as Marvin Gaye, Stevie Wonder, the Supremes, and Smokey Robinson and the Miracles.

The late 1960s brought massive unrest to the country and the worst race riot in Detroit's history. In 1967, Detroit was the site of one of 59 racial "disturbances" around the country, a tragedy in which more than 43 people were killed. The nightly news in cities throughout

the world showed a Detroit in flames, leaving a lasting impression on the country and a deep scar on the city's psyche.

The riots touched off an even greater exodus, the infamous "white flight" that left Detroit with a black majority in less than five years. By the 1970s, downtown had become a virtual desert after business hours. Controversial mayor Coleman Young, who ruled the city for two decades, once said you could shoot a displaced people during both the Great Depression and the 12th Street race riots of 1967. Over the years, visitors have reported ghostly sightings and other unfathomable occurrences on the fort's grounds.

· **The Majestic:** One of Detroit's finest entertainment centers, The Majestic (4140 Woodward Ave., 313/833-9700, www.majesticdetroit.com) consists of The Majestic Theatre, a spacious concert hall opened in 1915; The Majestic Stick, a smaller but equally well-respected live music venue; the Majestic Café, a well-regarded restaurant; and The Garden Bowl, a 16-lane bowling alley that's been active for a century. Supposedly, the complex is haunted by the ghost of Harry Houdini, who gave one of his final performances at The Majestic in 1926.

· **Masonic Temple:** Constructed in 1912 by George D. Mason, Detroit's grand Masonic Temple (500 Temple Ave., 313/832-7100, www.themasonic.com) is the largest in the world, boasting more than 1,000 rooms, not to mention a variety of secret staircases and hidden passages. Sadly, Mason spent so much money on the building's construction that he eventually went bankrupt, lost his wife, and subsequently jumped to his death from the roof of the temple. Since then, security guards and visitors alike have experienced cold spots, bizarre shadows, and inexplicable pranks, heard slamming doors that can't be explained, and even spotted the ghost of Mason himself.

· **Saint Andrew's Hall:** Once home to the St. Andrew's Society of Detroit, a group of upper-class Scottish Americans, Saint Andrew's Hall (431 E. Congress St., 313/961-6358 or 313/961-8961, www.saintandrewsdetroit. com) is now one of Detroit's most popular live music venues. Curiously, rapper Eminem got his start in the basement of Saint Andrew's, known as The Shelter. Supposedly, the basement is also home to a ghost who enjoys chasing visitors from the hall; some say that it might be one of the former tenants, who, given his Scottish roots, might prefer bagpipes to rap music.

· **2 Way Inn:** Founded in 1876, the 2 Way Inn (17897 Mt. Elliott St., 313/891-4925, www.2wayinn.com) is considered the oldest bar in Detroit. Both past and present owners of the property claim to have seen the cowboy-like ghost of Philetus Norris, a Union spy, archaeologist, and Yellowstone National Park superintendent that once lived and worked here.

· **The Whitney:** Built in 1894 by lumber baron David Whitney, The Whitney (4421 Woodward Ave., 313/832-5700, www. thewhitney.com) is now one of the city's fanciest fine-dining restaurants. Apparently, it's also haunted by the tuxedo-clad ghost of Whitney himself. According to witnesses, he tends to operate the elevator on his own and can often be heard washing and stacking dishes in the kitchen.

cannon down Woodward in those years without hitting a soul.

Today, some 3.9 million people call Detroit and its suburbs home. They comprise myriad ethnic groups, with more than 880,000 African Americans in the metropolitan area and the country's largest population of Bulgarians, Chaldeans, Belgians, and Arabs (the most outside the Middle East).

While the city has courted big business

almost since the first horseless carriage jounced awkwardly off the assembly line, Detroit has never been a major tourist destination. An active tourism bureau has attempted to change that, with frequent events for national and international media and an aggressive campaign to attract visitors from other parts of the country as well as Europe and Japan.

In 1996, the much-celebrated anniversary of the "birth" of the car turned an international spotlight on the city, with favorable reports in both the *New York Times* and *USA Today*. Detroit responded with a centennial bash and invited the entire world. In 2001, the city celebrated its third century with exhibitions, events, and a month-long riverfront party with visits that included both tall ships and the Temptations. Stevie Wonder led the homecoming concert, which attracted approximately one million people (ironically, more than the city's current population).

While city boosters don't expect flashy events such as these to erase the memories of Detroit in flames during the 1967 riots, they hope that they'll help to heal the wounds that have too long plagued the city—and perhaps ameliorate more recent troubles, such as Mayor Kwame Kilpatrick's 2008 resignation and subsequent felony conviction for obstruction of justice or, for that matter, the Michigan governor's 2013 declaration of a financial emergency for the city of Detroit.

Sights

ON THE WATERFRONT

Motown's earliest history was made on its waterfront, so a tour is a fitting start to any exploration of the city.

Hart Plaza

If it's a sunny day (regardless of the season), stroll the boardwalk near Hart Plaza and watch for one of the thousands of hulking freighters that traverse the Detroit River annually. Once, the waterfront, with its active port, was the city's livelihood. During the 20th century, however, Detroit turned its back on its former front door, choosing to erect faceless factories and anonymous office towers along its riverbanks instead of the more gracious green spaces popular during the previous century. Luckily, recent efforts have strived to correct the mistake: When completed, the **Detroit Riverfront** (www.detroitriverfront.org) will comprise a new harbor, a network of biking and jogging trails, and over five miles of public parks and plazas, linked by a continuous riverwalk.

For now, strollers can enjoy a three-mile stretch of the riverwalk and places like the expanded William G. Milliken State Park and the 14-acre Hart Plaza, a popular venue for summertime festivals and concerts. Opened in 1975 and named after the late U.S. Senator Philip Hart, Hart Plaza is the site of the breathtaking **Horace E. Dodge Fountain,** which was

designed in 1978 by Isamu Noguchi. This impressive fountain propels more than one million gallons of water per hour into the air via more than 300 streaming nozzles and jets. Another key landmark in Hart Plaza is the **Gateway to Freedom International Memorial to the Underground Railroad,** which was sculpted by Ed Dwight and dedicated in October 2001—in honor of both Detroit's tricentennial and its pivotal role as a 19th-century gateway for thousands of African American slaves seeking freedom in nearby Canada.

◖ GM Renaissance Center

Next to Hart Plaza is the gleaming **GM Renaissance Center** (100 Renaissance Center, 313/567-3126, www.gmrencen.com), known to Detroiters as Ren Cen. Soaring high into the sky, this fortress-like, 73-story hotel/office/retail complex dominates the Detroit skyline, with seven steel towers containing more than 5.5 million square feet of space, including a 1,300-room Marriott hotel, two foreign consulates, a fitness center, a four-screen movie theater, and dozens of restaurants and stores.

Of course, the road to the Ren Cen's present incarnation was rather rocky at best. The project was originally proposed by Henry Ford II, partially as a response to the 1967 riots. Ford—always a powerful name in Detroit—used his considerable influence to convince friends and foes alike to invest in the riverside

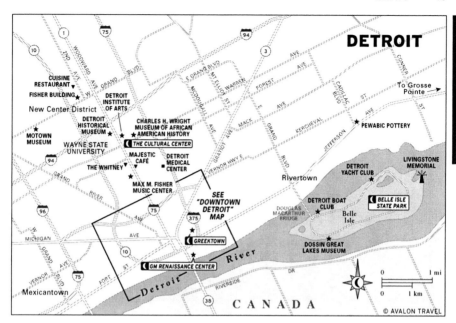

complex. With big-name retailers such as Gucci and Cartier, it was intended to draw suburbanites back to downtown Detroit. But it didn't work. The Ren Cen was a huge white elephant from the moment it opened in 1977. Designed by John Portman, best known for building hotel atriums, it was a confusing maze of circles and elevators that ultimately led nowhere. By 1983, many of the original retailers had pulled out and most of the investors had defaulted on their loans.

The center received a much-needed facelift and helpful new directional signs in the mid-1980s, but it never became the city's much-heralded savior. Through the 1980s and much of the 1990s, the Ren Cen was supported by various companies—including Ford, ANR Pipeline, and others—some of which have kept offices here. In 1996, however, it received a huge shot in the arm with General Motors' announcement that it had purchased the landmark to use as its new world headquarters. In a major boost for the city, GM moved the majority of its workers into the Ren Cen in 1999. A major internal reorganization followed, leaving the space a bit less confusing.

The Ren Cen is still one of the largest privately financed developments in U.S. history, with more than $380 million contributed by private investors. Representing a huge investment in the city's future, it is worth seeing on that basis alone. Once inside, you'll need a map to navigate. Otherwise, you can take a free one-hour tour (313/568-5624, noon and 2pm Mon.-Fri.) through this Detroit landmark. Tours, which are offered on a first-come, first-served basis, depart from the Pure Detroit store, situated on Level 1 of Tower 400, and feature sights like a world map carved in granite, a vintage auto collection, the world's tallest vertical glass sculpture, a tropical atrium overlooking the Detroit River, and breathtaking views of the Detroit and Windsor skylines.

Belle Isle State Park

At one time, 30 million tons of cargo were transported along the Detroit River, linking the city with more than 200 overseas ports.

Anna Scripps Whitcomb Conservatory, Belle Isle State Park

Nowadays, you can still feel the water's tug on Belle Isle, accessible via the Douglas MacArthur Bridge at East Jefferson Avenue and East Grand Boulevard. This 982-acre, 2.5-mile-long urban sanctuary, stranded a half mile out in the river, between Detroit and Windsor, Ontario, has been a public park since 1879, when the city purchased it for a now paltry $200,000 from the heirs of a wealthy local family.

Named after the then-governor's daughter, Isabelle Cass, it was designed in 1883 by Frederick Law Olmsted, the famous landscape architect known for his work on New York's Central Park. One of the city's most underrated (and often neglected) jewels, Belle Isle gets a little rowdy on summer weekends, when teenagers from surrounding neighborhoods cruise the narrow streets and pathways looking for action. Although patrolled by both mounted police and squad cars, it's not a safe place to be at night.

On weekdays, however, it's peaceful, especially off-season. Belle Isle is a haven for bird-watchers and for families who flock here to fish from the north and south piers, relax on Detroit's only swimming beach, and tour the vintage glass **Anna Scripps Whitcomb Conservatory** (313/821-5428, 10am-5pm Wed.-Sun., free), which features collections of ferns, orchids, cacti, and other plants. Kids will especially appreciate the small playground, the giant slide ($1 pp), the **Belle Isle Nature Zoo** (313/852-4056, 10am-5pm Wed.-Sun. May-Nov., 10am-4pm Wed.-Sun. Dec.-Apr., free), which oversees a one-acre deer enclosure, and the intriguing **Dossin Great Lakes Museum** (100 Strand Dr., 313/833-5538, www.detroithistorical.org, 11am-4pm Sat.-Sun., free), which traces the development of Great Lakes-area shipping from sailing vessels to modern freighters, many of which can still be seen from the riverfront.

Other visitors to Belle Isle come to jog, circle the island by bike, practice golf on the driving range and various greens, or just set up a picnic lunch under one of the gazebos and watch passing freighters. Boating enthusiasts, meanwhile, can wander around the

80-foot-tall marble **Livingstone Memorial Lighthouse,** which operated from 1882 to 1930, or check out the pleasure craft docked at the 1922 **Detroit Yacht Club.** Other curious historic structures include the 1908 **Belle Isle Casino,** the 1923 **James Scott Memorial Fountain,** the 1941 **International Peace Memorial,** and numerous other monuments. Admission to the island is free, though there has been an ongoing debate about charging a nominal admission to help defray maintenance costs.

It isn't the island's first controversy. Native Americans called Belle Isle "Rattlesnake Island" because of the number of snakes. Later, hogs were brought in by 18th-century settlers to destroy the rattlers, giving rise to the name Isle au Cochon ("Hog Island" in French) until 1845, when it was rechristened Belle Isle. Throughout its long history, the island has been used both as a dueling ground and as a place of quarantine for troops, most recently during the cholera epidemic of 1932. Since the early 1970s, four different groups—the Friends of Belle Isle, the Belle Isle Botanical Society, the Belle Isle Women's Committee, and the Friends of the Belle Isle Aquarium—have strived to protect the island, and in 2009, they joined forces to form the **Belle Isle Conservancy** (8109 E. Jefferson Ave., 313/331-7760, www.belleisleconservancy.org). In late 2013, its advocates went a step further by making it an official state park.

Pewabic Pottery

On Jefferson Avenue, not far from Belle Isle, is another oasis, **Pewabic Pottery** (10125 E. Jefferson Ave., 313/626-2000, www.pewabic.org, 10am-4pm Mon.-Fri.). Founded by Mary Chase Perry Stratton in 1903, this arts-and-crafts pottery is housed within a picturesque Tudor Revival building, now a National Historic Landmark. Best known for their innovative and iridescent glazes, shown to great advantage in the tiles commissioned for many of the city's civic and residential structures, Pewabic tiles can be found in the stunning 1929 art deco Guardian Building, several

downtown People Mover stations, and the Shedd Aquarium in Chicago.

Now a nonprofit ceramic arts center and a living museum, Pewabic continues to produce the handcrafted vessels and architectural tiles that brought it initial fame. Visitors peer into huge, fiery kilns on a self-guided tour during business hours. A landmark of Detroit's arts community, the pottery is a pilgrimage for potters and ceramic artists from around the country as well as the site of popular classes, workshops, and lectures for all ages. But don't look for the secret to the pottery's lustrous glaze—Stratton took it to the grave, leaving her successors to carry on with only an approximation of the original formula.

Riverboat Tours

For a terrific view of Detroit's skyline, consider taking a ride on the Detroit River, the world's busiest international waterway. **Diamond Jack's River Tours** (313/843-9376, www.diamondjack.com, tours 1pm and 3:30pm Thurs.-Sun., $17 adults, $15 seniors over 60, $13 children 6-16, children under 6 free) offers two-hour narrated riverboat cruises June-August. There are two departure points for these informative tours: Detroit's Rivard Plaza and Wyandotte's Bishop Park. Be advised, however, that tours are available on a first-come, first-served basis; in other words, individual reservations are not accepted, so it's prudent to arrive at least 30 minutes, if not an hour, before departure time.

DOWNTOWN DETROIT

Woodward Avenue marks the entrance to the city's official downtown business district. This area may be quiet after business hours, but during the day, it hops with office workers who toil in the banks, insurance companies, and other corporations.

The first stop on any architectural tour is the **Wayne County Building** (600 Randolph St.) on the east end of Cadillac Square, an early example of the Roman Baroque Revival style in Michigan. Built from 1897 to 1902, it's one of the oldest buildings in the city. Look up to see its ornamental cornices—they depict General "Mad" Anthony Wayne conferring with the Indians. (General Wayne, incidentally, served during the Revolutionary War and negotiated a treaty that claimed all the lands between the Ohio and Mississippi Rivers for the United States.) Not surprisingly, it was listed on the National Register of Historic Places in 1975.

History buffs may also appreciate the art deco **Guardian Building** (500 Griswold St., www.guardianbuilding.com), a 40-story, Aztec-inspired structure that has been designated a National Historic Landmark. Friendly guards in the 1929 superstructure are usually pleased to share tidbits about the breathtaking building or point you in the right direction for a self-guided tour of its Pewabic-accented interior.

Meanwhile, the buildings of Woodward Avenue cast a long shadow over **Harmonie Park** (www.harmoniepark.com), the center of an area once known as Paradise Valley, an impoverished African American neighborhood that was also a hotbed of jazz and other artistic activity from the 1920s to the 1950s. If Woodward's desolation threatens to overwhelm you, this elegant enclave—nestled between Grand Circus Park, Randolph Street, and Gratiot Avenue—will restore your hope in the city's future. New energy has transformed a formerly deserted area into the city's hottest nightspot. Much of the credit goes to local architectural firm Schervish Vogel Merz, who believed in the area long before anyone else saw a future in its warehouse-style buildings and vintage storefronts. Today, Harmonie Park is surrounded by pubs, galleries, and airy artists' lofts.

Theater District

Not far from Harmonie Park lies the official entrance to Detroit's Theater District. Once the city's most exclusive address, the neighborhood known as Brush Park had deteriorated almost to the point of no return before local boy Mike Ilitch—owner of the nationwide Little Caesars Pizza chain as well as the Detroit Tigers baseball and Detroit Red Wings hockey teams—stepped in and bought the aging **Fox**

Theatre (2211 Woodward Ave., 313/471-3200 or 313/471-6611, www.olympiaentertainment. com) in 1988.

What followed was a painstaking and often slow $8 million restoration that eventually returned the gaudy yet glamorous structure to its original glory. The 5,048-seat Fox is truly a marvel of 1920s architecture. Built in 1928 by William Fox, it was designed in the style of an Arabian tent. The exotic Thai-Byzantine style borrows motifs from a range of cultures, including Persian, Burmese, Indian, Thai, and Chinese. There are gold-leafed, hand-stenciled walls, marble-finish pillars, gold-tusked elephants, winged lions, a sunburst ceiling, and dreamlike decorative figures throughout. The lobby is six stories high, with 300,000 sparkling glass jewels, loads of brass, and a 13-foot, two-ton stained-glass chandelier. No wonder it was listed on the National Register of Historic Places in 1985 and, following the successful restoration, designated a National Historic Landmark in 1989.

Today, the Fox is one of the nation's most successful theater operations, with almost nightly presentations, including touring Broadway musicals, big-name concerts, restored film epics, and other special events. You can't miss the 125-foot multicolored neon marquee, which stretches to the 10th floor of the Fox office building. And here's a bit of trivia: During the 1920s, the Fox was the first theater in the United States to sell candy on-site.

Spurred by the resounding success of the Fox, other theaters soon followed. One contrast to the cavernous Fox is the intimate **Gem & Century Theatres** (333 Madison Ave., 313/963-9800, www.gemtheatre.com), a joint cabaret-style venue with 450 seats. Founded in 1903 by a women's group hoping to have an "uplifting influence on the community," the Gem degenerated into a burlesque and adult movie theater before ultimately closing in 1978. Soon afterward, foresighted businessman Chuck Forbes, owner of most of the city's vintage theaters, restored it as a complement to the Fox and a stop for national comedy acts, small plays, and musical revues. It reopened in

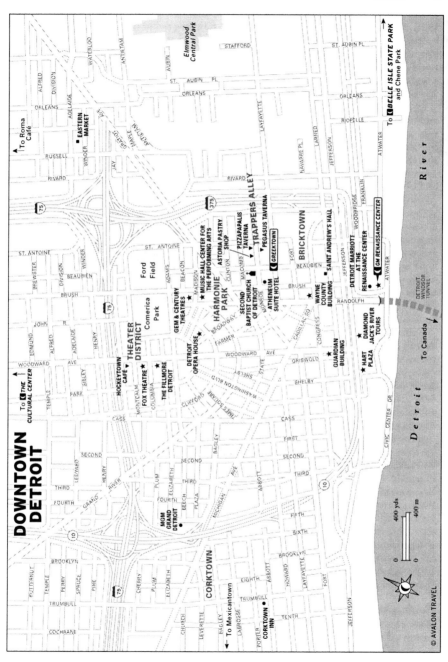

DOWNTOWN
DETROIT

© AVALON TRAVEL

1991. Threatened by the new Comerica Park ballpark—home to the Detroit Tigers—it was moved to its present location in 1997. As the world's heaviest building ever to be moved on wheels, it even made the pages of *Guinness World Records.*

Luciano Pavarotti and Dame Joan Sutherland were just a few of the big names who jetted into Motown in 1996 to attend the opening of the restored **Detroit Opera House** (1526 Broadway St., 313/237-7464, www.michiganopera.org). Designed in 1922 by C. Howard Crane as a vaudeville stage, the 7,000-square-foot theater served as a parking garage for most of the 1970s. David Di Chiera, the former university professor who founded the Michigan Opera Theatre in 1971 as a way to bring opera to kids, did the seemingly impossible when he raised $36 million for the opera's new 2,700-seat home. Today, it acts as an important cultural resource, luring Broadway musicals as well as opera and ballet productions.

Other area theaters include **The Fillmore Detroit** (2115 Woodward Ave., 313/961-5451, www.thefillmoredetroit.com), a live music venue built in 1925 as the State Theatre, and the **Music Hall Center for the Performing Arts** (350 Madison St., 313/887-8500, www.musichall.org), built in 1928 by the widow of auto baron John Dodge for the production of "legitimate" theatrical productions. Its stage has been graced by luminaries such as Lucille Ball, W. C. Fields, Martha Graham, Ella Fitzgerald, Lillian Hellman, and others. Music lovers, meanwhile, flock to the **Max M. Fisher Music Center** (3711 Woodward Ave., 313/576-5100 or 313/576-5111, www.dso.org), which, since 2003, has housed The Music Box, a 450-seat performance hall, as well as the acoustically perfect Orchestra Hall, which was built in 1919 and has long been home to the acclaimed Detroit Symphony Orchestra.

◖ Greektown

Once a pioneer farm and now the city's best-known ethnic area, **Greektown** (www.greektowndetroit.org) has long been a bright spot

downtown and one of the few districts that jump after midnight. Despite the unfortunate failure of the Trappers Alley shopping and entertainment complex that once thrived here, this restored stretch of Monroe Street still attracts both natives and visitors. (It also attracts parking enforcement officers, so if you park at one of the plentiful metered spots around Monroe, be sure to bring plenty of change.)

At the core of it all is a Greek neighborhood that dates back to 1915. Although most of the original residents have moved to the suburbs and the majority of restaurants and bakeries have gone upscale, you'll still find a few coffeehouses where old-timers gather to drink strong coffee or sip sweet retsina and play cards. One original grocery remains: Open the rusty screen door of the **Athens Grocery & Bakery Co.** (527 Monroe St., 313/961-1149, 9:30am-midnight Mon.-Thurs. and Sun., 9:30am-2am Fri., 10am-2am Sat.), and you'll walk past windows full of neatly arranged loaves of bread, sinfully sweet Greek pastries, and shiny tins of pungent imported olives.

Other highlights include two of Detroit's most notable churches. **Old St. Mary's Church** (646 Monroe St., 313/961-8711, www.oldstmarysdetroit.com), one of the city's most beautiful Roman Catholic structures, dates to 1841, serves as Detroit's third-oldest Catholic parish, and is, curiously, the city's first German church. Meanwhile, the **Second Baptist Church of Detroit** (441 Monroe St., 313/961-0920, www.secondbaptistdetroit.org, free) was established in 1836 by several former slaves who had left the First Baptist Church due to discrimination against African Americans. Once a stop on the Underground Railroad, Second Baptist also established the first school for black children, and its congregation has included the country's first black schoolteacher, several presidents of the Detroit NAACP, and the first African American to receive the Nobel Peace Prize.

◖ The Cultural Center

Head north along Woodward Avenue from downtown, and you'll run right into the

Cultural Center, part of **Midtown Detroit** (www.detroitmidtown.com). Bordered by bustling **Wayne State University** to the west and the **Detroit Medical Center** to the east, this is where you'll find a plethora of art galleries, performance venues, shops, and restaurants, plus most of the city's art and civic museums. It's also home to the **International Institute of Metropolitan Detroit** (111 E. Kirby St., 313/871-8600, www.iimd.org), which, besides offering citizenship classes and other educational programs, presents the inexpensive International Cafe, the longstanding International Festival in early October, and the Ethel Averbach International Doll Collection, supposedly the world's largest collection of dolls dressed in native costumes. Roughly a block away from the International Institute, you'll also encounter the main branch of the **Detroit Public Library** (5201 Woodward Ave., 313/481-1300, www.detroit.lib.mi.us, noon-8pm Tues.-Wed., 10am-6pm Thurs.-Sat.), which opened in 1921 and now features a variety of engrossing collections, such as the Burton Historical Collection, which contains thousands of volumes, pamphlets, and papers that shed some light on the histories of Detroit and Michigan from the 1600s to the present, and the equally comprehensive E. Azalia Hackley Collection of African Americans in the Performing Arts, which encompasses rare books, manuscripts, photographs, recordings, and sheet music that explore everything from early 19th-century plantation life in the American South to the Motown Recording Company.

Here, in the Cultural Center, you can also wander the "Streets of Old Detroit" (or at least an idealized version of them) in the basement of the **Detroit Historical Museum** (5401 Woodward Ave., 313/833-1805, www.detroithistorical.org, 9:30am-4pm Tues.-Fri., 10am-5pm Sat.-Sun., free). You'll trudge along irregular cobblestones that once lined city streets past re-creations of barber shops, grocery stores, and other vintage businesses. The display, which opened in 1951 and has since been updated, traces several periods of Detroit history.

The permanent exhibit "Frontiers to Factories" traces the city's history from a trading post to an industrial giant, with a walk-in diorama from the 1750s, a railway station, and a mock turn-of-the-20th-century exposition. Other highlights of the collection include the Glancy Train display, one of the world's largest; special exhibits about Detroit's leaders, symbols, and entertainment venues; and an exhibition simply named "America's Motor City," which traces the history of the car, the city, and the people who changed the world when they came to work here. The exhibit's highlight is the "body drop," a segment of a 1953 assembly line in which the outer shell of a later-model Cadillac is lowered from the ceiling onto an engine body set up on an eye-level platform. It was taken from the assembly line at the now-demolished Clark Street Cadillac plant. Following an extensive renovation and the 2012 reopening, visitors can also experience an expanded "Doorway to Freedom: Detroit and the Underground Railroad" exhibit as well as five new permanent exhibitions: the "Gallery of Innovation," the "Allesee Gallery of Culture," the "Kid Rock Music Lab," "Legends Plaza," and "Detroit: The Arsenal of Democracy."

Detroit has always been a blue-collar town, yet city founders amassed enough green during the heyday of the auto industry to fund what eventually became one of the country's finest art museums. The **Detroit Institute of Arts** (DIA, 5200 Woodward Ave., 313/833-7900, www.dia.org, 9am-4pm Tues.-Thurs., 9am-10pm Fri., 10am-5pm Sat.-Sun., $8 adults, $6 seniors, $5 college students, $4 children 6-17, children under 6 and area residents free) attracts more than 500,000 visitors each year. The sometimes-confusing 100-plus galleries contain some of the greatest art treasures of the world, including works by Van Gogh, Rodin, Rembrandt, Bruegel, and other masters.

The museum strives to present an encyclopedic collection, with a multicultural scope that traces creativity in all of its forms, from prehistory through the present. Important collections include the French Impressionist, Italian (the largest outside Italy), German Expressionist, African, Asian, Native American, and 20th-century. It's worth hunting for the museum's generally accepted best works, including Rodin's pensive masterpiece, *The Thinker;* Bruegel's *The Wedding Dance* (look closely and you may see some remnants of paint on the bulging codpieces; they were once painted over); Van Eyck's tiny treasure, *Saint Jerome in His Study;* and Rembrandt's enlightened *The Visitation.*

While the building may seem to be full of art made by and for the ruling class, the city's workers have the last laugh in the breathtaking *Detroit Industry* frescoes. Mexican muralist Diego Rivera captured the droning monotony of the assembly line in 27 huge panels surrounding the museum's central courtyard. Rivera spent nine months in Detroit from 1932 to 1933 before unveiling the series to great controversy. A visionary Edsel Ford stood up to virulent criticism of the Mexican socialist's frescoes, which were damning in their innate criticism of capitalism. Many city leaders wanted the walls whitewashed as soon as the scaffolding came down, but Ford stood firm, defending the murals, which, unlike another series in New York's Rockefeller Center, were saved.

Relax and rest your feet with a cup of java or something stronger in the **Kresge Court** (11am-3pm Tues.-Thurs., 11am-9pm Fri., 11am-4pm Sat.-Sun.), a soaring green and light-filled space modeled after Florence's Bargello Palace, or enjoy soups, salads, sandwiches, and other treats in **CaféDIA** (11:30am-2:30pm Tues.-Thurs., 11:30am-2:30pm and 4pm-9pm Fri., 11:30am-3pm Sat.-Sun.). If you're visiting on a weekend, stick around long enough to take in a movie at the museum's acclaimed 1,150-seat **Detroit Film Theatre** (313/833-3237 or 313/833-4005), which offers important premieres by new and established directors and is one of the few venues in the city to show restored, rarely seen classics in their correct aspect ratios. *Variety* called it "the best buy for cineastes in America."

Art lovers will also enjoy the **Museum of Contemporary Art Detroit** (MOCAD, 4454 Woodward Ave., 313/832-6622, www.mocadetroit.org, 11am-5pm Wed. and Sat.-Sun., 11am-8pm Thurs.-Fri., $5 adults, students and children under 12 free), a cavernous museum that, in addition to presenting fascinating exhibitions, offers a unique gift shop, a small café, and assorted lectures, concerts, films, and literary readings. Another highlight of the city's Cultural Center is the **Michigan Science Center** (5020 John R St., 313/577-8400, www.mi-sci.org, 9am-3pm Wed.-Fri., 10am-6pm Sat., noon-6pm Sun., $13-24 adults, $10-20 children 2-12, children under 2 free), which reopened to the public in July 2001. The center now includes a digital planetarium, two theaters, one science stage, the state's only IMAX dome theater, and areas devoted to motion, life sciences, matter, energy, waves, and vibration.

History buffs, meanwhile, may relish a chance to visit the **Charles H. Wright Museum of African American History** (315 E. Warren Ave., 313/494-5800, www.thewright.org, 9am-5pm Tues.-Sat., 1pm-5pm Sun., $8 adults, $5 seniors 62 and over and children 3-12, children under 3 free), which hosts the annual African World Festival and serves as the world's largest institution devoted to exploring the African American experience. Meanwhile, Wayne State University's recently renamed **Gordon L. Grosscup Museum of Anthropology** (4841 Cass Ave., Old Main, 1st Fl., 313/577-2598, http://clasweb.clas.wayne.edu/anthromuseum, 10am-4pm Mon.-Thurs., 10am-2pm Fri., free), which was established in 1958, houses both permanent and temporary exhibits, many of which feature artifacts from various sites throughout Detroit, from Fort Wayne to Belle Isle to the GM Renaissance Center.

Another intriguing site is the **First Congregational Living Museum** (33 E. Forest Ave., 313/831-4080, www.friendsoffirst.com, 9am-5pm daily, free), which is housed within the First Congregational Church of Detroit and its Albert Kahn-designed Angels' Wing Community House. Visitors to the church may appreciate strolling among the ornate religious paintings that line the walls of the 120-year-old sanctuary; just be advised that this is an active church, which means that it's best to visit on weekday afternoons (2pm-4pm Tues.-Fri.). While here, you may also be able to experience the "Underground Railroad Flight to Freedom Tour" (hours vary Tues.-Sat., $12 adults, $10 children 3-17, $8 seniors 62 and over, children under 3 free), a reenactment during which participants are shackled and led to liberation by a "conductor." Because this experience involves volunteer actors, however, the church staff requires a minimum of 20 participants for each tour.

For a different aspect of Detroit's history, head to the **Hellenic Museum of Michigan** (67 E. Kirby St., 313/871-4100, www.hellenicmi.org, noon-4pm Sat., donation suggested), which opened in 2010 in the hopes of becoming a modern-day version of the "Mouseion" (House of the Muses) of ancient Alexandria. Although still in its early stages, the museum will eventually, through the use of artifacts, photographs, oral histories, and personal documents, present the numerous artistic and intellectual achievements of Hellenic culture from ancient times to the present. It also aims to chronicle the considerable struggles, triumphs, and contributions of the Greek immigrants that settled throughout Michigan, including Detroit. During the summer months, the museum presents traditional Greek music, dancing, and cuisine during their weekly Kefi Nights, which usually take place on Thursday (6pm-10pm).

Even children will appreciate the Cultural Center, which, besides the fascinating Michigan Science Center, is home to the **Detroit Children's Museum** (6134 2nd Ave., 313/873-8100), the country's third-oldest children's museum. Founded in 1917, this kid-friendly attraction is temporarily closed to the public due to lack of funding, and only open to Detroit-area public schools.

New Center

Situated about a mile north of the Cultural Center, the commercial district known as **New Center** (www.newcenterplace.com), which was named in part as an optimistic effort to replace the city's ailing downtown, was once best known for its most famous resident, General Motors. The twin towers of GM's corporate headquarters housed thousands of workers; for decades, its lavish 1st-floor showrooms were filled year-round with the latest models, hot off the drawing boards located in the upstairs offices.

Much to the chagrin of GM's employees and executives, the corporate headquarters were surrounded by a once-fine neighborhood that had become seedy and derelict. With the clout and bankroll to pull off what few other companies in the world could at the time, GM spent millions upon millions buying, rehabbing, and reselling the old homes in the surrounding neighborhood—renamed New Center. The idea was to spruce up the company's surroundings, draw its employees and other middle- and upper-income families back downtown, and, hopefully, spur more area redevelopment.

While the New Center neighborhood slowly began to improve, GM ended up leaving the

Detroit's New Center area

area anyway and moving downtown to the Ren Cen in 1999. Since then, the GM building, which has since been renamed Cadillac Place, has struggled to attract tenants. Among those who have moved in are local health care offices as well as various government agencies of Michigan.

Of the New Center's two main attractions, the **Fisher Building** (3011 W. Grand Blvd.) is perhaps the most interesting. Even if you're not an architecture fan, it's worth seeing for the dazzling ceiling mosaics alone. The Architectural League of New York recognized the Fisher Building as the world's most beautiful commercial structure shortly after it was built in 1928. Albert Kahn, one of the city's best-known architects, made lavish use of expensive materials, including 420 tons of bronze, marble, Minnesota granite, and 24-karat gold. Today, the building's 30-story central tower and two 11-story wings house the Fisher Theatre, shops, restaurants, and office space.

Dwarfed by the Fisher Building and Cadillac Place is the diminutive **Motown Museum** (2648 W. Grand Blvd., 313/875-2264, www.motown-museum.org, 10am-6pm Tues.-Sat. Sept.-June, 10am-6pm Mon.-Fri., 10am-8pm Sat. July-Aug., $10 adults, $8 seniors 62 or older and children 5-12, children under 5 free). Known to many across the country as "Hitsville U.S.A.," this is where the Motown Sound exploded from the now-legendary Studio A and soon had teenagers around the country "Dancin' in the Streets."

Berry Gordy Jr. bought the unremarkable two-story house in 1959 as a fledgling songwriter with a dream of managing singers. Today, the state historic site looks much as it would have in the early 1960s, with an office and tape library filled with reel-to-reel tape machines, company manuals, and newspaper clippings. The 2nd floor re-creates Gordy's 1959-1960 apartment, where he and his staff would spend nights packing records to ship to radio stations around the country. The museum's most prized display, however, is the original Studio A, where top tunes such as "Stop

in the Name of Love" and "My Girl" were recorded. Diana Ross and the Supremes, Smokey Robinson and the Miracles, Martha Reeves and the Vandellas, Gladys Knight and the Pips, Lionel Ritchie and the Commodores, The Temptations, the Four Tops, the Marvelettes, Marvin Gaye, Stevie Wonder, and the Jackson Five all recorded in this studio during their early careers. Other artifacts on display in the two museum buildings (at its zenith, the company owned seven buildings along West Grand Boulevard) include rare photos, gold records, flashy costumes, and similar memorabilia. Just be advised that the museum is closed on major holidays and that cameras and cell phones are not allowed inside.

Mexicantown

The smell of fresh tortillas baking at the **La Jalisciense Tortilla Factory** (2650 Bagley St., 313/237-0008, www.tortillamundo.com) leads hungry diners and curious visitors to Bagley Street, the main thoroughfare of the city's Mexican district. Located about five miles from downtown on the city's southwest side, the neighborhood is divided by I-75, so there's an eastern and western side, with shops, restaurants, and homes on both. Here's where you'll find colorful Mexican *mercados* and see elderly Mexican women, heads covered with an old-fashioned lace mantilla, praying with their rosaries in one of the historic churches, including **Ste. Anne de Detroit Catholic Church** (1000 Ste. Anne St., 313/496-1701, www.ste-anne. org, free), the city's oldest, founded in 1701. During the summer, the area hosts a popular outdoor market on Sunday where you can pick up fresh chili peppers and other spicy souvenirs.

The Mexican restaurants grouped along the streets around Bagley provide the area's main income and job base. Here, you'll find authentic Mexican cuisine, such as salt-rimmed margaritas, soft-shell tacos full of spicy meat and onions, and soft, flaky *sopaipillas* that rival the best south of the border. Queen of them all is the **Xochimilco Restaurant** (3409 Bagley St., 313/843-0179, 11am-2am daily, $4-14), where Mexican art and the eyes of God cover the walls, and where weekend waits can stretch to over an hour. Many flock to Xochimilco for the inexpensive lunch specials, though other fans of Mexican fare may prefer less-crowded competitors, such as the **Mexican Village Restaurant** (2600 Bagley St., 313/237-0333, www.mexicanvillagefood.com, 11am-10pm Sun.-Thurs., 11am-midnight Fri.-Sat., $5-21).

Entertainment and Events

NIGHTLIFE

When the sun goes down, the lights come on around the city. No matter what your style is, Detroit offers plenty of places where you can party and, more importantly, listen to good music, from alternative sounds at **Saint Andrew's Hall** (431 E. Congress St., 313/961-6358 or 313/961-8961, www.saintandrews-detroit.com, show times and ticket prices vary) to smooth jazz at the longstanding **Baker's Keyboard Lounge** (20510 Livernois Ave., 313/345-6300, www.theofficialbakerskeyboardlounge.com, 11am-midnight Tues.-Thurs., 11am-2am Fri., 4pm-2am Sat., 1pm-midnight Sun.), which claims to be the world's oldest jazz club. Another popular hangout is **Flood's Bar & Grille** (731 St. Antoine St., 313/963-1090, www.floodsdetroit.com, 4pm-midnight Mon., 3pm-2am Tues.-Fri., 7pm-2am Sat.-Sun., $5-10 cover), which features jazz, R&B, sweet soul, or karaoke nightly.

CASINOS

In late 1996, city voters approved a controversial referendum permitting casino gambling within city limits. More than 15 years later, three casinos are now open—and remain controversial. Whether gambling is the struggling inner city's angel or devil is still being decided, not only at the craps tables but also in the hearts of residents.

For those who enjoy rolling the dice, options include **MGM Grand Detroit** (1777 3rd St., 877/888-2121, www.mgmgranddetroit.com), a flashy, art deco palace that draws its inspiration from the Hollywood of yesteryear and offers nearly 4,000 slot and video poker machines, roughly 100 table games, and a nonsmoking poker room. Beyond gaming activities, MGM

Grand also features a full-service hotel, a sports pub, two Wolfgang Puck restaurants, a luxurious spa, four unique bars, a pulsating nightclub, and plenty of live entertainment. Motown in all its glory provides the theme for the locally owned **MotorCity Casino Hotel** (2901 Grand River Ave., 866/752-9622, www.motorcitycasino.com), housed in a former Wonder Bread warehouse and connected by skywalks to downtown restaurants and parking. In addition

MORE THAN MOTOWN

Detroit has always been a complex town. Its many facets have spawned many monikers – not the least of which honors its status as the birthplace of a groundbreaking musical style. But Motown legends like Martha Reeves, Diana Ross, Smokey Robinson, Mary Wells, Gladys Knight, and Stevie Wonder aren't the only musically oriented folks to have spent their formative years in and around Detroit. Southeastern Michigan has also nurtured a brood of well-known rock 'n' rollers and hip-hop stars, including:

- Sonny Bono
- Alice Cooper
- Eminem
- Glenn Frey
- Bill Haley
- Madonna
- Ted Nugent
- Iggy Pop
- Kid Rock
- Bob Seger

to a smoke-free poker room, 59 table games, and more than 2,900 slot and video poker machines, the MotorCity Casino encompasses a comfortable hotel, a relaxing spa, a roomy concert hall, and several dining options, from award-winning Iridescence to a delectable buffet. The **Greektown Casino-Hotel** (1200 St. Antoine St., 313/223-2999, www.greektowncasino.com), meanwhile, is the city's most spacious, with Las Vegas-style gaming and easy access to the city's liveliest neighborhood. As with its competitors, it, too, provides a stylish hotel, live entertainment, and various dining and nightlife options.

THE ARTS

Productions at the 5,048-seat **Fox Theatre** (2211 Woodward Ave., 313/471-3200 or 313/471-6611, www.olympiaentertainment.com, show times and ticket prices vary) include touring Broadway musicals, big-name concerts, restored film epics, and other special events. The tiny and jewel-like **Gem & Century Theatres** (333 Madison Ave., 313/963-9800, www.gemtheatre.com, show times and ticket prices vary) is a cabaret-style venue that has, since being relocated in the late 1990s, featured national comedy acts, small plays, and musical revues; today, it's a popular spot for weddings and other special events. The restored **Detroit Opera House** (1526 Broadway St., 313/237-7464, www.michiganopera.org, show times and ticket prices vary), home of the Michigan Opera Theatre, attracts full-scale productions of opera, ballet, and Broadway musicals.

Other area theaters include **The Fillmore Detroit** (2115 Woodward Ave., 313/961-5451, www.thefillmoredetroit.com, show times and ticket prices vary), a live music venue built in 1925 as the State Theatre; the **Music Hall Center for the Performing Arts** (350 Madison St., 313/887-8500, www.musichall.org, show times and ticket prices vary), which features contemporary ballet, live concerts, music festivals, and more; and the **Fisher Theatre** (3011 W. Grand Blvd., 313/879-5433 or 313/872-1000, www.broadwayindetroit.com), which opened as a movie and vaudeville house in

1928 and now features both modern and classic Broadway shows. For classical music, consider the **Max M. Fisher Music Center** (3711 Woodward Ave., 313/576-5100 or 313/576-5111, www.dso.org, show times and ticket prices vary), home to the acclaimed Detroit Symphony Orchestra.

FESTIVALS AND EVENTS

Detroit hosts numerous events and celebrations throughout the year, including January's **North American International Auto Show** (COBO Center, 1 Washington Blvd., 248/643-0250 or 313/877-8777, www.naias.com, $13 adults, $7 seniors 65 and over and children 7-12, children under 7 free), which still offers the world a firsthand look of what cars will look like in the near and distant future. In early April, Greektown comes alive with the annual **Detroit Greek Independence Day Parade** (http://detroitgreekparade.blogspot.com, free), which is typically held on Monroe Street, the main thoroughfare of this historic enclave.

In 2009, the longstanding Detroit Belle Isle Grand Prix, which, much to the chagrin of naturalists, used to take over the beloved island every Labor Day weekend, was indefinitely suspended, due to lack of funding. To the delight of many, however, this popular event returned to Belle Isle in the spring of 2013. Now, the weekend-long **Chevrolet Detroit Belle Isle Grand Prix** (313/748-1800 or 866/464-7749, www.detroitgp.com) occurs in late May or early June and features various races on Belle Isle's 2.3-mile road course, considered one of the most challenging in the world.

In late June, the St. Nicholas Greek Orthodox Church holds the annual **Opa! Fest** (760 W. Wattles Rd., Troy, 248/362-9575, www.opafest.com, $2 pp, children under 12 free), a weekend filled with Greek music, traditional Greek folk dancing, Greek arts and crafts, cooking demonstrations, and, of course, Greek cuisine, from kabobs and gyros to pastries and wine. Another popular summertime event is the **African World Festival** (313/494-5824, free), which has been hosted by the **Charles H. Wright Museum of African**

ELMORE LEONARD'S MOTOR CITY

Born in New Orleans, Elmore John Leonard Jr. (1925-2013), the son of a General Motors employee, spent the bulk of his adolescent and teenage years in Detroit. Following high school, he served in the U.S. Navy for three years. After graduating from the University of Detroit with an English and philosophy degree, he began to write ad copy for clients like Chevrolet. Eventually, however, his love of fiction proved to be too great an urge to resist.

While maintaining his advertising job, he began to pen Western stories, popular in the 1950s. When the Western market shrank a decade later, Leonard decided to focus on a full-time writing career. Soon, he'd crafted his first crime novel, *The Big Bounce* (1969). Over the ensuing years, he continued to write crime novels (often set in his hometown), gradually gaining a loyal cult following. Adapting several of his stories into screenplays helped to fund his fiction career – until the publication of two bestsellers propelled *Time* to christen him the "Dickens from Detroit" in 1984.

For the next three decades, Leonard, who lived in a Detroit suburb until his death, continued to write best-selling crime novels and short stories, some of which have become popular films and television shows, including *Get Shorty* (1995), *Jackie Brown* (1997), *Out of Sight* (1998), *Killshot* (2008), *Justified* (2010-present), and *Freaky Deaky* (2012). Even his Western tales have made a resurgence: In 2007, Russell Crowe and Christian Bale starred in *3:10 to Yuma*, the second adaptation of his eponymous short story.

If you're curious about Leonard's sharp-tongued take on gritty Detroit, visit the author's official website (www.elmoreleonard.com) or consider perusing the following titles:

UNKNOWN MAN NO. 89 (1977)
When a skillful Detroit process server is hired to search for a missing stockholder, he becomes the unwitting target of a lethal triple-cross.

THE SWITCH (1978)
Hoping to make some easy ransom money, two ex-cons kidnap the wife of a Detroit developer who, unfortunately for them, has no desire to get her back.

CITY PRIMEVAL (1980)
A dedicated homicide detective strives to stop a psychopathic murderer in the Motor City.

TOUCH (1987)
A former Franciscan monk with faith-healing powers finds it difficult to be a saint in the city.

FREAKY DEAKY (1988)
After his fishy suspension from the Detroit police force, a determined sergeant must uncover a web of scams, perpetrated by an ex-con, a former Black Panther, a movie dynamite expert, and an alcoholic auto industry heir.

OUT OF SIGHT (1996)
A career thief forms an unlikely relationship with a sexy U.S. marshal, which leads them both from sunny Florida to the gritty streets and posh suburbs of Detroit.

MR. PARADISE (2004)
When two roommates – a lingerie model and an escort – get involved with a retired Detroit-based lawyer, murder, greed, and pandemonium ensue.

UP IN HONEY'S ROOM (2007)
In World War II-era Detroit, a young U.S. marshal befriends a free-spirited American woman in the hopes that she'll lead him to her husband – a German-born butcher who's giving shelter to German prisoners of war, perhaps even the marshal's latest target.

American History (315 E. Warren Ave., 313/494-5800, www.thewright.org, 9am-5pm Tues.-Sat., 1pm-5pm Sun., $8 adults, $5 seniors 62 and over and children 3-12, children under 3 free) for the past three decades. Usually taking place in mid-August, this beloved festival features world music, jazz and blues, a folk village, an international marketplace, ethnic cuisine, traditional dances, and other tantalizing diversions.

Over Labor Day weekend, there's at least one event worth attending. From Hart Plaza to Cadillac Square, the **Detroit Jazz Festival**

(313/447-1248, www.detroitjazzfest.com, free) presents a wide array of open-air concerts and a world-class selection of music masters—the largest free jam in the world. Festival attendees can also experience lively interviews, panel discussions, and presentations by musicians, journalists, and jazz radio hosts. Throughout the year, festival organizers and the Detroit public school system offer a "Jazz Infusion Program," designed to teach students improvisation and other jazz-related skills in an effort to support the city's vital jazz community and ensure its survival.

Shopping

GM RENAISSANCE CENTER

Downtown shoppers can spend at least a couple of hours browsing the boutiques inside the Ren Cen (100 Renaissance Center, 313/567-3126, www.gmrencen.com). Options run the gamut, from **The Runway** (313/568-7977, 10am-6pm Mon.-Fri., 11am-4pm Sat.-Sun.), which sells high-end men's and women's apparel, to the charming **Renaissance 500 Shoppe** (313/259-6510, 7am-5:30pm Mon.-Fri.), where the friendly staff provides fine tobacco products and other specialty items.

EASTERN MARKET

There is one place in the city where old and young, Eastsider and Westsider, black and white meet. Bring your wagon or grocery bag to the historic **Eastern Market** (2934 Russell St., 313/833-9300, www.detroiteasternmarket. com), between Mack and Gratiot Avenues, on a Saturday morning, and you'll find a fragment of old Detroit, a colorful cornucopia of smells,

sights, and sounds. In a city that's known great cycles of boom and bust, Eastern Market is as perennial as the fruit and flowers it sells.

Built on the site of an early hay and wood market, this bustling, six-block area near Greektown has lured Detroiters since 1891. Shoppers come to buy meat, cheese, produce, fruit, and flowers from large, open-air stalls and wholesale/retail specialty shops. Many wholesalers are the descendants of the Belgian, German, and Polish farmers who frequented the market generations ago, or the Italian and Lebanese merchants who began catering to the booming city in the 1920s.

Saturdays are busiest, when the farmers market runs 6am-4pm and thousands of shoppers pour into the area to browse, bargain, and buy among goods that range from fresh chitlins to fresh cilantro. Highlights include the flower stalls (the market is the largest bedding center in the world) and the aromas at **Germack's,** the oldest pistachio importer in the United States.

Sports and Recreation

SPECTATOR SPORTS

The Motor City boasts more professional sports teams than most major U.S. cities, and Detroiters are among the country's most loyal fans, with thousands cheering on the home teams at Lions football, Pistons and Shock basketball, Tigers baseball, and Red Wings hockey games. Most are played at sparkling modern suburban stadiums, much like their counterparts across the country.

Historic Tiger Stadium, which once stood at Michigan Avenue and Trumbull Street, was demolished in 2009. Legendary and longtime home to the **Detroit Tigers** (http://detroit.tigers.mlb.com), it was replaced in April 2000 by the glitzy **Comerica Park** (2100 Woodward Ave., 313/962-4000 or 866/668-4437), where baseball games usually take place April-October. While it will never be Tiger Stadium, Comerica Park certainly has its fans. With a

family-friendly philosophy that includes a Ferris wheel and a pedestrian museum, it has attracted city and national attention as one of the best of the new breed of ballparks. The location in the heart of the vintage Theater District is also prime.

Just east of Comerica Park is the relatively new **Ford Field** (2000 Brush St., 313/262-2013), which is home to the **Detroit Lions** (www.detroitlions.com) and typically features football games September-December. Basketball lovers, meanwhile, can seek out the NBA's **Detroit Pistons** (www.nba.com/pistons) or the WNBA's **Detroit Shock** (www.wnba.com/shock) at **The Palace** (6 Championship Dr., Auburn Hills, 248/377-0100, www.palacenet.com) November-April, and, of course, hockey fans can cheer on the **Detroit Red Wings** (http://redwings.nhl.com) at **Joe Louis Arena** (19 Steve Yzerman Dr., 313/396-7000

© SUSAN MONTGOMERY/123RF.COM

Comerica Park

or 313/471-6606, www.olympiaentertainment. com) October-April.

BIKING

If you're looking for a leisurely bike ride, head to **William G. Milliken State Park and Harbor** (1900 Atwater St., 313/396-0217, free), which was formerly known as Tri-Centennial Park and now offers a bike path not far from the Detroit River. Experienced bikers, on the other hand, should head beyond the city limits, where the **Highland Recreation Area** (5200 E. Highland Rd., White Lake, 248/889-3750, www.michigan.gov/dnr, 8am-10pm daily) offers 16 miles of trails that make up some of the area's most challenging mountain biking routes. Another option is **Pinckney State Recreation Area** (8555 Silver Hill Rd., Pinckney, 734/426-4913, www.michigan.gov/dnr), home to the 17-mile Potawatomi Trail, which has been ranked in the nation's top 10 routes and also caters to hikers and, in winter, cross-country skiers. To enter the two recreation areas, an annual Recreation Passport is required for both residents ($11 vehicles, $5 motorcycles) and nonresidents ($30.50 vehicles or motorcycles); luckily, though, these passports will allow you access to all of the Michigan state parks and recreation areas that charge a fee.

BOATING AND FISHING

Given Detroit's proximity to the Detroit River, Lake Erie, and Lake St. Clair, it might come as no surprise that boating and fishing are popular activities here. If you don't have a boat of your own, simply contact the **Michigan Charter Boat Association** (MCBA, 800/622-2971, www.michigancharterboats.com), which can help you locate and join sailing excursions and fishing charters. Of course, if don't want to stray too far, head to **William G. Milliken State Park and Harbor** (1900 Atwater St., 313/396-0217, free), which offers easy access to shore fishing alongside the Detroit River.

WINTER ACTIVITIES

As with the rest of Michigan, Detroit certainly gets its share of snow and ice during the winter months. So, if you enjoy cold-weather diversions, you're in luck. Ice skating, ice fishing, sledding, tobogganing, cross-country skiing, and downhill skiing are all popular in and around the city. Ice skaters, for example, can head to **Campus Martius Park** (800 Woodward Ave., www.campusmartiuspark.org, 7am-10pm), a 2.5-acre public square and year-round entertainment venue that also features a world-class rink during the winter. Apparently, even national and Olympic ice-skating champions have performed here. Another option for wintertime recreationists is **Lake Erie Metropark** (32481 W. Jefferson, Brownstown, 734/379-5020, www.metroparks.com, 6am-10pm daily, $7/vehicle daily, $20-30/vehicle annually), a 1,607-acre recreation area that lies about 27 miles south of downtown Detroit. Here, cross-country skiers can embrace 4.25 miles of marked, groomed trails; ice-fishing enthusiasts can search for perch, bass, and other species on Lake Erie; and sledders can plummet down a large hill near the wave pool complex.

Accommodations

Detroit offers hotels, motels, and inns to suit all budgets. Although most downtown accommodations are of the business-class, hotel-chain variety, you'll even find a few Victorian-style inns and casino resorts.

UNDER $150

Close to downtown attractions, the **Hotel St. Regis** (3071 W. Grand Blvd., 313/873-3000 or 855/408-7738, www.hotelstregisdetroit.com, $94-144 d) provides 124 renovated rooms and suites, free wireless Internet access, valet parking ($20 daily), a 24-hour business center, and an on-site restaurant, La Musique (6am-10pm Mon.-Thurs., 8am-11pm Fri.-Sat., 8am-10pm Sun.). West of Detroit's stadiums and theaters, the 150-room **Corktown Inn** (1331 Trumbull St., 313/496-1400, www.corktowninn.com, $70-100 d) is a solid option for budget-conscious travelers who need little more than clean beds, laundry services, free parking, wireless Internet access, and proximity to Detroit's main attractions.

$150-300

If you don't mind paying a bit more, then consider the 🄲 **Atheneum Suite Hotel** (1000 Brush Ave., 313/962-2323 or 800/772-2323, www.atheneumsuites.com, $199-259 d), downtown's best all-suite hotel. Located in the heart of Greektown, it borrows classical motifs from the surrounding neighborhood in its 174 luxury suites, all with separate living rooms, marble bathrooms, free wireless Internet access, and other convenient amenities. Wheelchair-accessible suites are also available here.

Another solid option is the **Detroit Marriott at the Renaissance Center** (GM Renaissance Center, 400 Renaissance Dr., 313/568-8000 or 888/236-2427, www.marriott.com, $179-299 d), which provides terrific views of the Detroit River as well as easy access to the Ren Cen's shops and restaurants, Detroit's three casinos, and the tunnel to Windsor, Canada. Here, you can also enjoy high-speed Internet access, a fitness center, a business center, and an on-site restaurant.

For traditional chain lodgings, consider the **Hilton Garden Inn Detroit Downtown** (351 Gratiot Ave., 313/967-0900, www.hiltongardeninn.com, $159-229 d), set within the Harmonie Park neighborhood, only a block from Comerica Park and Ford Field. Housing 198 rooms and suites, the Hilton also offers free wireless Internet access, a business center, two on-site restaurants, a fitness center, an indoor pool, and plenty of wheelchair-accessible features. Another mid-range option is the **Holiday Inn Express Hotel & Suites Detroit Downtown** (1020 Washington Blvd., 313/887-7000 or 888/233-0353, www.ihg.com, $150-180 d), which lies halfway between the MGM Grand Detroit and Greektown Casino-Hotel, and within walking distance of Campus Martius Park. Besides affordable guest rooms, the Holiday Inn also features suites with fully equipped kitchens, plus a fitness center, an indoor heated pool, a 24-hour business center, valet parking ($20 daily), free high-speed Internet access, and a complimentary breakfast bar. You might also try **Courtyard Detroit Downtown** (333 E. Jefferson Ave., 313/222-7700 or 888/236-2427, www.marriott.com, $159-219 d), with 260 oversized rooms, free wireless Internet access, an extensive health club, an enormous indoor pool, and an outdoor aboveground tennis court/running track that offers terrific views of the city's surrounding vintage architecture.

CASINO RESORTS

For even more amenities, consider staying at one of Detroit's three downtown casino resorts. The shimmering 🄲 **MGM Grand Detroit** (1777 3rd St., 888/646-3387 or 877/888-2121, www.mgmgranddetroit.com, $249-499 d) houses an enormous gaming space, a full-service spa, pampering hotel rooms, live entertainment, four unique bars, a lively nightclub, and several dining options, including the Wolfgang Puck Pizzeria & Cucina as well as Wolfgang Puck Steak. The **MotorCity Casino Hotel** (2901 Grand River Ave., 866/752-9622, www.motorcitycasino.com, $223-332 d) also promises more than Las Vegas-style games, including a 24-hour fitness center, a luxurious spa, live concerts, varied dining options, and 400 stylish, state-of-the-art rooms and suites. Even Greektown has its own resort, the **Greektown Casino-Hotel** (1200 St. Antoine St., 313/223-2999 or 877/424-5554, www.greektowncasino.com, $99-249 d), which offers several restaurants, a video poker lounge, a wide range of gaming tables and slot machines, and amenities like ergonomic desks, plush bedding, and free parking.

Food

GREEKTOWN

Greektown is a delightful place come mealtime, and most Detroiters have their favorite Greektown restaurant. Top choices include the **New Parthenon** (547 Monroe St., 313/963-8888, www.newparthenon.com, 11am-3am daily, $9-24), which serves various salads, sandwiches, kabobs, gyro platters, and seafood dishes, and the upscale **(** **Pegasus Taverna** (558 Monroe St., 313/964-6800, www.pegasustavernas.com, 11am-1am Mon.-Thurs., 11am-3am Fri.-Sat., 11am-midnight Sun., $7-32), which offers specialties like a tart *avgolemono* (chicken lemon soup), flaky spinach pie, *pastitsio* (Greek macaroni), and flaming *saganaki* cheese, lit with a flourish and a cry of "Opa!" from the waiter. Afterward, many diners wander over to the popular **(** **Astoria Pastry Shop** (541 Monroe St., 313/963-9603, www.astoriapastryshop.com, 8am-midnight Sun.-Thurs., 8am-1am Fri.-Sat., $2-11) for baklava and other Greek and European pastries laid out neatly behind gleaming glass counters. Incidentally, the Pegasus Taverna has a second location in St. Claire Shores, while the Astoria Pastry Shop also offers its treats to the residents of Royal Oak, so even in the suburbs, you can sample the flavors of Greektown.

Of course, not everything worth seeing in Greektown is Greek. **PizzaPapalis Taverna** (553 Monroe St., 313/961-8020, www.pizzapapalis.com, 11am-1am daily, $5-24) is where Motown meets the Windy City. Only the name is Greek: Deep-dish pies are the specialty. Meanwhile, **(** **Fishbone's** (400 Monroe St., 313/965-4600, www.fishbonesusa.com, 6:30am-midnight Sun.-Thurs., 6:30am-1am Fri.-Sat., $9-65) is a New Orleans-inspired eatery that opened in the mid-1980s and has been jammed ever since. It serves up surprisingly authentic gumbo and jambalaya, in addition to ribs, steaks, seafood, and sushi, and you can usually expect live music on Friday and Saturday nights. Given its popularity, it's no wonder that there are also locations in Southfield and St. Claire Shores.

THEATER DISTRICT

Detroit's impressive Theater District is home to more than just gorgeously restored entertainment venues; it also boasts a decent array of restaurants, which, depending on the hours, might be ideal for a post-game or pre-show meal. Located behind the Comerica Park scoreboard, the **Elwood Bar & Grill** (300 Adams Ave., 313/962-2337, www.elwoodgrill.com, 11am-2pm Mon.-Tues., 11am-8pm Wed.-Sat., $6-9) might just be Detroit's most recognizable art deco-style diner. Built in 1936 by local architect Charles Noble, relocated in 1997, and subsequently renovated, the Elwood is, not surprisingly, a popular spot for sports fans, particularly given its menu items, which range from chicken wings and Coney-style hot dogs to patty melts and club sandwiches. Another equally casual option is the **(** **Hockeytown**

CONEY CUISINE

Philly may have the cheese steak and Chicago its deep-dish pie, but Detroit has *the* Coney Island. No, not the amusement park – the hot dog. Detroiters take their coneys very seriously, downing thousands of these hot dogs annually. Curiously, the name Coney Island serves simultaneously as both a destination and a dish.

Family-owned and operated since 1917, **American Coney Island** (114 W. Lafayette, 586/219-0995, www.americanconeyisland. com) is the place where a wiener with skin, beanless chili, onions, and mustard was first called "one with everything." Although this beloved 24-hour eatery now also serves soups, salads, desserts, and spinach pie, it's the dogs that lure a clientele ranging from cops on the beat to fur-clad suburbanites grabbing a bite after a show at the Fox Theatre. American Coney Island has garnered the respect of a long list of celebrities, too, including Michigan governors, famous musicians and athletes, and well-known actors like Bill Cosby, Tim Allen, and Jeff Daniels.

Cafe (2301 Woodward Ave., 313/471-3400, www.hockeytowncafe.com, 11am-close Mon.-Sat., Sunday hours vary, $8-19). Though not far from the Fox Theatre, this bustling sports bar is, as the name implies, more popular among sports fans headed to or from the nearby Comerica Park and Ford Field. During hockey season, patrons can even hop the restaurant's free shuttles to the Joe Louis Arena. Diners here can anticipate frequent drink specials; vittles like chicken wings, salads, pizza, ribs, and burgers; and a host of high-definition TVs broadcasting a variety of sporting events. Curiously, there are also gluten-free options on the menu, from nachos to breadless sandwiches.

EASTERN MARKET

After shopping in the Eastern Market, head over to the **Roma Café** (3401 Riopelle St., 313/831-5940, www.romacafe.com, 11am-10pm Mon.-Fri., 11am-11pm Sat., $14-29), Detroit's oldest Italian restaurant, established in 1890. While classic dishes such as gnocchi, lasagna, eggplant parmigiana, and tiramisu abound here, you'll also find treats like breaded frog legs, filet mignon, and broiled whitefish.

WOODWARD AVENUE

If you get hungry while exploring the Cultural Center, stop by the ◖ **Majestic Café** (4140 Woodward Ave., 313/833-9700, www.majesticdetroit.com, 11am-10pm Wed.-Thurs., 11am-midnight Fri.-Sat., 10am-10pm Sun., $8-22), an eclectic eatery offering hummus, fish tacos, baked ziti, soft-shell crab po-boys, and more. It packs in the Wayne State University and Detroit Medical Center crowds at lunch. For a decidedly fancier experience, make a reservation at ◖ **The Whitney** (4421 Woodward Ave., 313/832-5700, www.thewhitney.com, 8am-10pm Mon.-Fri., 5pm-10pm Sat., 11am-2:30pm and 4pm-8pm Sun., $28-79), Detroit's grandest restaurant, housed in an ornate 120-year-old mansion and offering live entertainment on weekends, plus exquisite dishes such as beef Wellington, stuffed lobster, roasted lamb rack, and bourbon-glazed salmon. A prix-fixe theater menu is also available. In addition, with a 48-hour advance reservation, you can enjoy high afternoon tea on weekdays, and the trendy **Ghostbar** is open 5pm-close Monday-Saturday.

NEW CENTER DISTRICT

Even the New Center district has its own gem: the ◖ **Cuisine Restaurant** (670 Lothrop Rd., 313/872-5110, www.cuisinerestaurant.com, 5pm-close Tues.-Sun., $22-32), situated behind the Fisher Building. If you're willing to spend a fair amount, treat yourself to one of

Chef Paul Grosz's progression menus ($50-80 pp), which might include dishes like white and green asparagus, creamed Maine lobster with leeks and tapioca, almond-crusted soft-shell crabs, roasted Alaskan halibut, wild sturgeon with potato gnocchi, and strawberry Charlotte. The restaurant also offers vegetarian options and a superb wine list.

Information and Services

INFORMATION

For free information about Detroit, consult the **Detroit Metro Convention & Visitors Bureau** (211 W. Fort St., Ste. 1000, 313/202-1800 or 800/338-7648, www.visitdetroit.com, 9am-5pm Mon.-Fri.). The two daily newspapers, the **Detroit News** (www.detnews.com) and the **Detroit Free Press** (www.freep.com) are supplemented by a wide variety of suburban dailies and weeklies, as well as the weekly **Detroit Metro Times** (www.metrotimes.com). The *Metro Times* is the city's first—and most successful—alternative rag, with thoughtful reporting on a variety of civic and social issues, extensive entertainment listings (a great place to check out your options on any given night), and consciousness-raising (if not eyebrow-raising) classifieds and want ads. It's distributed freely at bins throughout the city and suburbs. Another good read is **Hour Detroit** (www.hourdetroit.com), a tabloid-size, full-color magazine that's full of thought-provoking and entertaining editorials.

Local radio and television stations, such as Detroit's ABC affiliate **WXYZ** (www.wxyz.com), are also excellent sources for regional information. Pick up a copy of the *Detroit News* or check the website (www.detnews.com) for a list of channels.

SERVICES

As a major urban center, Detroit has no shortage of necessary services, from banks to mailing centers to grocery stores. The metropolitan area boasts several post offices, including one inside the Ren Cen. For locations and hours, contact the **United States Postal Service** (USPS, 800/275-8777, www.usps.com).

Dial **911** for emergency police, fire, or ambulance assistance. In nonemergency situations, contact the **Detroit Police Department** (1301 3rd St., 313/596-2200 or 313/596-1300, www.detroitmi.gov); you can also dial 311 within the city limits. Remember, too, that the area code for Detroit and Dearborn telephone numbers is 313, while the area codes for Oakland County (including Birmingham, Royal Oak, Pontiac, and most of the northern suburbs) are 248 and 947.

For medical assistance, you'll find several hospitals in the metropolitan area. One option is the **Detroit Medical Center** (DMC, 888/362-2500, www.dmc.org), which has a number of facilities in the vicinity.

Getting There and Around

Most international travelers arrive by air, while American tourists tend to come via train, bus, or car.

GETTING THERE
By Plane

The **Detroit Metropolitan-Wayne County Airport** (DTW, 1 Detroit Metropolitan Airport Tram, 734/247-7678, www.metroairport.com), also known as the Detroit Metro Airport, spreads out over some 7,000 acres, 21 miles southwest of the city in Romulus, just off I-94 and Merriman Road. With 12 airlines, including 4 foreign, Detroit Metro offers service to more than 160 nonstop destinations. Consult the website for current carriers, which range from Air Canada to United.

Sedan or limo service from the airport to downtown hotels and area suburbs (and vice versa) is available by reservation. Typically, a one-way ride costs $31-98, depending on the destination. For more information, contact **Metro Airport Taxi** (800/745-5191, www.metroairporttaxi.org), **Metro Airport Limo** (734/322-0240 or 800/654-1215, www.dtwmetrotaxi.com), **Metroride** (248/666-0222 or 800/320-1683, www.detroitmetroairport.com), or **Rendezvous Limousine** (800/875-4667, www.rendezvous-limo.com).

Detroit Metro also has many car rental services: some on-site, others off-site but accessible via a dedicated shuttle service. For details, consult **Avis** (800/331-1212, www.avis.com), **Budget** (800/527-0700, www.budget.com), and **Enterprise** (800/325-8007, www.enterprise.com), or peruse the listings on the DTW website.

By Train

Via the Michigan Services route, **Amtrak** (800/872-7245, www.amtrak.com) offers convenient daily service to five metro area stops: Dearborn, Detroit, Royal Oak, Birmingham, and Pontiac. The downtown station is located at 11 West Baltimore Avenue in the New Center, while the suburban Dearborn stop is situated at 16121 Michigan Avenue.

By Bus

Greyhound (800/231-2222, www.greyhound.com) serves downtown Detroit (1001 Howard St., 313/961-8011, 5:30am-1:30am daily). Be extra careful at this station—it's not located in the best part of town. Daytime arrivals and departures are always a good idea.

By Car

Many travelers arrive in the Detroit area via car. While several federal and state highways make it easy to navigate the Motor City, most motorists rely on interstates to reach Detroit. If you're headed from Flint, for instance, take I-75 South to downtown Detroit; without traffic, the 69-mile trip usually takes about an hour. From Toledo, on the other hand, head north on I-75 for about 61 miles; without traffic, you should arrive in downtown Detroit in roughly an hour. From Lansing, meanwhile, take I-96 East, which passes through Farmington Hills and Southfield en route to Detroit's Mexicantown; this particular route covers about 90 miles and normally requires about 80-90 minutes of driving. I-94 is another handy route into the city; from Ann Arbor to the west, it's roughly 45 miles (or 45 minutes, without traffic) via I-94 East to Detroit, while from Port Huron to the northeast, it's approximately 63 miles (or an hour, without traffic) via I-94 West to Detroit. If you're headed from Chicago, you can also utilize I-94 East to reach Detroit; without traffic, the 283-mile trip normally takes about four hours. Just be advised that, en route from the Windy City, you'll encounter the Indiana Toll Road.

GETTING AROUND
By Car

Detroit, not surprisingly, is full of freeways. I-75 is the major north-south thoroughfare, with I-96, I-696, and I-94 heading east-west. Avoid traveling any of these routes during rush hours (generally 6am-10am and 3pm-7pm) or allow plenty of extra time. It's wise to seek out alternate routes such as I-275, which splits off from I-696, and to pick up a map of the area to ensure that you don't get lost (which is an easy thing to do).

Of course, if you've arrived in Detroit via plane, train, bus, boat, or some other means, and you don't have a car of your own, there's no need to worry. Rental car companies—including Avis, Budget, and more—can be found at the Detroit Metro Airport. Likewise, you can also rely on taxis to navigate the city. **Checker Cab** (313/963-7000, www.checkercab-det. com, $2.50/pickup, $1.60/mile), for instance, has been driving passengers around the greater Detroit area since 1921. From the airport to downtown hotels, it typically costs about $40 per trip, while it's roughly $10 from downtown Detroit to the New Center district. Typically, a waiting charge will run you about $15 per hour or more.

Whether you rely on your own or someone else's vehicle, just remember that seat belts are required by Michigan law; in other words, all drivers, front-seat passengers, and children 8-15 years old must wear seat belts while in a moving vehicle. Otherwise, law enforcement officials can (and often do) stop and ticket motorists solely for not being buckled up.

Mass Transit

Most would agree that mass transit in Detroit is a joke. (This is the city that invented the car, after all.) The **Detroit Department of Transportation (DDOT)** is the state's largest transit system; it serves Detroit and 25 suburban communities. DDOT buses and bus stops are recognizable by their trademark green and yellow colors.

© JERRY BERNARD/123RF.COM

Detroit People Mover

Buses operate on 50 routes during the day and evenings from 6am until approximately 1am; 14 of the most popular routes operate 24 hours daily. Consult **DDOT** (313/933-1300 or 888/336-8287, www.ci.detroit.mi.us/ddot, one-way $1.50 adults, $0.75 students, $0.50 seniors) for routes and schedules.

While downtown, you can also take advantage of the **Detroit People Mover** (313/224-2160 or 800/541-7245, www.thepeoplemover.com, 6:30am-midnight Mon.-Thurs., 6:30am-2am Fri., 9am-2am Sat., noon-midnight Sun.), which admittedly never quite lived up to the high expectations. Still, it's a handy way to travel, with a bird's-eye view of the city from its elevated track. For 75 cents, you'll get a 15-minute ride along a three-mile track that circles the heart of the business district. Even if you don't ride, it's worth a visit to check out the 13 People Mover stations, which boast works by local artists. The Detroit People Mover operates through the city's notable areas, including the Civic Center, Greektown, and the Theater District, with easy access to major attractions, such as the GM Renaissance Center and the Joe Louis Arena.

Windsor, Ontario

A city of 211,000, Windsor sits along the southern banks of the Detroit River, just across from the Motor City. "Civilized" is the word that comes to mind when Detroiters talk about Windsor. Although separated only by a river, this Canadian city has a virtually nonexistent crime rate, a full plate of excellent restaurants, and a friendly and civic-minded populace who are happy to welcome Yanks. Detroiters have long shuttled back and forth to enjoy Windsor's restaurants, casinos, European-style shops, terrific riverfront views, and, yes, strip clubs.

SIGHTS

The **Windsor Wood Carving Museum** (850 Ouellette Ave., 519/977-0823, www.windsorwoodcarvingmuseum.ca, 10am-5pm Tues.-Fri., 10am-4pm Sat., donation suggested) offers a glimpse into historical carvings as well as contemporary work by some of Canada's finest craftspeople. The expansive one-room museum allows for close-up viewing of most of the pieces. **The Park House Museum** (King's Navy Yard Park, 214 Dalhousie St., Amherstburg, 519/736-2511, www.parkhousemuseum.com, 11am-4pm daily June-Aug., 11am-4pm Mon.-Fri. Sept.-May, $2 adults, $1.50 seniors, $1 children), meanwhile, has the unique distinction of being the oldest house in the Windsor area

and the oldest house from Detroit. The house was built near the mouth of the Rouge River in Detroit in the 1790s, but when the city was turned over to the Americans with the signing of the Jay Treaty, Alexander MacKintosh, a loyalist to the crown, moved the house to Amherstburg in 1796.

SHOPPING

Wander Ouellette Avenue, the main drag, and the narrow streets surrounding it. Shops are full of imported clothing and books (both new and used, many with British publishers), and the T-shirt stands are ubiquitous. One standout is **Shanfields-Meyers** (188 Ouellette Ave., 519/253-6098, www.shanfields.com, 10am-5pm daily), a family-owned business that opened in 1946 and now houses a sparkling array of crystal, including a whole room devoted to Waterford, and a wide selection of discounted china and gifts.

ACCOMMODATIONS AND FOOD
Accommodations
Windsor is full of nice hotels, including the **Windsor Riverside Inn** (333 W. Riverside Dr., 519/977-9777 or 800/267-9777, www.windsorriversideinn.com, $105-159 d), which is

a view of the Ambassador Bridge

conveniently located near downtown Windsor and the Detroit River and offers spectacular views of the Detroit skyline. It also features pet-friendly rooms, a fitness center, an indoor pool and sauna, a 24-hour business center, complimentary Internet access, and free parking. For an equally affordable stay, try the pet-friendly **Travelodge Hotel Downtown Windsor** (33 E. Riverside Dr., 519/258-7774, www.travelodge.com, $95-150 d), which offers free wireless Internet access, a fitness center, a heated indoor pool, an on-site restaurant, and proximity to Caesars Windsor.

Of course, if you're looking for a bit more luxury, consider staying at **Caesars Windsor** (377 E. Riverside Dr., 800/991-7777, www.caesarswindsor.com, $110-233 d) itself, the city's premier gambling resort. Boasting 758 luxurious rooms and suites in two towers that overlook the Detroit River, Caesars also provides amenities like full concierge service and complimentary valet parking. It doesn't hurt that you'll also have easy access to various table

games and slot machines, a world-class poker room, live concerts and comedy shows, several stylish bars, upscale shops, a soothing spa, an indoor pool, a fully equipped gym with incredible views, and several restaurants, from Taza, a Mediterranean grill, to Neros, a superb steakhouse.

Food

While the shopping is good in Windsor, it doesn't compare to the eating. Top restaurants include **The Cook's Shop Restaurant** (683 Ouellette Ave., 519/254-3377, http://cooksshoprestaurant.wordpress.com, 5pm-10pm Tues.-Thurs. and Sun., 5pm-11pm Fri.-Sat., $15-24), a tiny basement eatery where everything is homemade, including the melt-in-your-mouth gnocchi, tortellini, and other pastas prepared tableside on a rolling cart. Another option, **The Mini** (475 W. University Ave., 519/254-2221, 11:30am-10pm Tues.-Fri., 5pm-10pm Sat., 4pm-8pm Sun., $7-14) started out with one tiny room (hence the name) and then expanded as the restaurant's Vietnamese cuisine and fruit slushes caught on with diners from Windsor and across the way.

INFORMATION

For more information about Windsor, consult **Tourism Windsor, Essex, Pelee Island** (333 W. Riverside Dr., Ste. 103, Windsor, Ontario, 519/255-6530 or 800/265-3633, www.tourismwindsoressex.com, 8:30am-4:30pm Mon.-Fri.).

GETTING THERE AND AROUND

While Windsor has its own airport—the **Windsor International Airport** (YQG, 3200 CR-42, 519/969-2430, www.yqg.ca)—most visitors will probably be making a day trip from Detroit via car. Two routes connect Detroit and Windsor: the **Ambassador Bridge** (www.ambassadorbridge.com, one-way $5 passenger vehicles and motorcycles, $10 buses) and the **Detroit-Windsor Tunnel** (www.dwtunnel.com, one-way to Windsor $4.75 passenger and commercial vehicles, $8.50 buses, one-way to Detroit $4.50 passenger and commercial vehicles, $8.50 buses). Claustrophobes tend to opt for the bridge, though the tunnel is faster and more direct.

If you don't have your own car, you can always rent a vehicle or hire a taxi or sedan at the Detroit Metro Airport. **Checker Cab** (313/963-7000, www.checkercab-det.com, $2.50 per pickup, $1.60 per mile), for instance, charges about $46 for a one-way trip from the airport to downtown Windsor, while, for the same trip, **Metro Airport Taxi** (800/745-5191, www.metroairporttaxi.org) usually charges passengers around $75, which includes airport fees and toll charges.

Just remember that this is an international border, and nowadays, U.S. citizens must confirm both proof of identity and proof of citizenship (by using, for instance, a driver's license and a birth certificate) in order to enter Canada. Unfortunately, returning to the United States will require a valid U.S. passport.

The Suburbs

Ironically, the same fast cars that made the Motor City what it was in its heyday are also what crippled it. Bigger and better cars, and more and more efficient freeways only served to take Detroiters farther and farther away from the core city. Most suburbs are bedroom communities that bear little interest for the visitor. Some exceptions include Hamtramck, a Polish neighborhood north of downtown Detroit; Dearborn, where Henry Ford was born and eventually inspired what has become one of the state's largest tourist attractions; Royal Oak, home to the Detroit Zoo; Birmingham, an enclave of chic boutiques and fine art galleries; and Grosse Pointe, where Lake Shore Drive still boasts some of the area's finest homes.

◖ HAMTRAMCK

"A Touch of Europe in America," reads the sign approaching **Hamtramck** (www.hamtramck.com), a Polish stronghold since World War I. Given that its residents have stubbornly withstood annexation, this curious community has survived as a "city within a city," 2.5 square miles completely within Detroit city limits.

Named for a German-French Canadian colonel who served during the post-Revolutionary Indian Wars, the strange-sounding hamlet was settled as a village of mostly German farms in 1901, but a new Dodge auto factory and its promise of jobs swelled the population from 3,589 to 45,615 between 1910 and 1920—the largest increase anywhere in the United States. Many were Polish immigrants, earning

Hamtramck the nickname "Little Poland." Today, the auto plant is closed and the Polish population has dropped from 90 percent to about 40 percent (the slack is taken up by Albanians and African Americans), but the nickname and culture remain.

Sights and Shopping

Drive along Joseph Campau Street, Hamtramck's main drag, and you'll find Polish bakeries, Polish bookstores, Polish clubs, and shops hawking Polish sausage. There's even a tribute at the corner of Belmont and Joseph Campau Streets to the Polish pope, John Paul II, who visited this ethnic enclave in the mid-1980s. Stop at the **Polish Art Center** (9539 Joseph Campau St., 313/874-2242 or 888/619-9771, www.polartcenter.com, 9:30am-6pm Mon.-Sat., 11am-3pm Sun.) for unusual goods such as folk art rugs, leaded glass, Ukrainian-decorated eggs, and *szopkas,* intricate Nativity scenes made of tinfoil. Afterward, take a tour of the **Saint Florian Roman Catholic Church** (2626 Poland St., 313/871-2778, www.stflori-anparish.org), one of the last of the old Polish churches. Founded in 1907 and completed in 1926, this stately church now serves hundreds of faithful parishioners, including Polish, Albanian, and Asian residents, among others.

Detroiters have long known about the old-world charms of Hamtramck. Joseph Campau's glass storefronts have a vintage 1930s feel, full of Polish imports, discount clothing, and baked goods and meats. Hamtramck's quirky 1930s flair and cheap rents have attracted artists such as potter/jeweler Marcia Hovland and film-makers Chuck Cirgenski and Janine Menlove. Hollywood-backed *Polish Wedding* (1998), a movie starring Claire Danes, Lena Olin, and Gabriel Byrne, was filmed here in late 1996. With the new wave of artists and filmmakers have come urbane coffeehouses, late-night alterna-tive-music cafés, and colorful studios and shops that add a new hipness to this old-world enclave.

Food

Many Polish suburbanites return to Hamtramck with their families on weekends to sip *czarnina* (duck's blood soup), linger over *nalesniki* (crepes), and consume pierogies (filled dumplings) before heading home with loaves of fresh pumpernickel or rye and a few Polish pastries, such as *paczki* (plump jelly doughnuts), to enjoy later. Highlights of Polish Hamtramck include the **New Palace Bakery** (9833 Joseph Campau St., 313/875-1334, www.newpalace-bakery.com, 6am-6pm Mon.-Sat.), the most popular of the many bakeries, and the **Polonia Restaurant** (2934 Yemans St., 313/873-8432, www.polonia-restaurant.net, 11am-8pm Mon.-Thurs., 11am-9pm Fri.-Sat., 1pm-7pm Sun., $5-9), housed in a former 1930s food co-op.

Getting There

Well known locally, Hamtramck can be hard to find for the visitor. To get here from down-town Detroit, follow I-375 North to I-75 North, take the Holbrook Street exit, turn right onto Holbrook, and then turn left onto Joseph Campau Street. Without traffic, this six-mile trip usually takes about 15 minutes.

DEARBORN

Home to Ford's international headquarters and the largest collection of Arabic-speaking peoples in the United States, Dearborn is rightly known as "the town that Ford built." After all, there was little here but farmland when Henry Ford was born in a small white farmhouse at the corner of Ford Road and Mercury Drive—a house that you can now see at The Henry Ford's acclaimed Greenfield Village.

Sights
ARAB AMERICAN NATIONAL MUSEUM

While in Dearborn, make time for at least a taste of its Arabian culture. Most of Dearborn's Arab citizens live in the neighborhoods that line Warren and Dix. (The Dix neighborhood lies in the shadow of the Ford Rouge Plant, one of the largest factories in the world.) Its working-class residents are more than 90 percent Arab, primarily from Yemen. The south end boasts signs that are in both English and Arabic, headscarves are common on women, and many men wear traditional skullcaps. The restaurants and shops along Dix offer sights and sounds heard in the Arabian peninsula, including a call to prayer broadcast five times daily from a local mosque. So, while here, take some time to visit the fascinating **Arab American National Museum** (13624 Michigan Ave., 313/582-2266, www.arabamericanmuseum. org, 10am-6pm Wed.-Sat., noon-5pm Sun., $8 adults, $4 seniors, students, and children 6-12, children under 6 free), the first and only museum in the United States devoted to Arab American history and culture. Here, through the use of art, artifacts, documents, and photographs, you'll see several permanent exhibits that explore Arabian culture, the experiences of Arabian immigrants coming to and living in America, and the influence of Arab Americans and their organizations on the American way of life. In addition, you'll encounter rotating exhibits, which can range from student art displays to immersive multimedia exhibitions that illustrate the anger, frustration, ebullience, and hope associated with the Arab Spring uprisings.

◖ THE HENRY FORD

Today, Dearborn is best known to tourists as the location of **The Henry Ford** (20900 Oakwood Blvd., 313/982-6001 or 800/835-5237, www.hfmgv.org), a favorite field trip for local schoolchildren and one of the state's biggest tourism draws. In the adjacent **Greenfield Village** (9:30am-5pm daily mid-Apr.-Oct., 9:30am-5pm Fri.-Sun. Nov., $24 adults, $22 seniors 62 and over, $17.50 children 5-12, children under 5 free), Henry gathered buildings and other structures in an attempt to show how America grew from an agrarian to an industrial society. It's a charming—if disconcerting—time machine, a patchwork quilt of unrelated people and places, where a 16th-century English Cotswold cottage sits a few hundred yards from an 18th-century New England saltbox. Other features include Ford's childhood home, Thomas Edison's Menlo Park laboratory, and a working 19th-century farm.

Ford sent his pickers across the Midwest and New England to assemble enough artifacts to fill the 12-acre **Henry Ford Museum**

(9:30am-5pm daily, $17 adults, $15 seniors 62 and over, $12.50 children 5-12, children under 5 free) next to the village. Inside is one vast collection after another, including several presidential limousines (including President Kennedy's and Ronald Reagan's), the world's greatest holdings of 19th-century farm and kitchen tools (the old washing machines are a stitch), a fine grouping of American furniture, and many artifacts that trace the evolution of the electric lightbulb (Edison was a great friend of Ford's; the complex was originally called the Edison Institute).

Worth the price of admission alone is the excellent exhibit known as "The Automobile in American Life," which nostalgically shows the car's effect on the American landscape. There's a 1950s McDonald's sign, complete with oversized golden arches; a 1946 diner from Marlboro, Massachusetts, where an egg salad sandwich cost 15 cents; a VW camper van, complete with a handy awning; and a Holiday Inn guest room, circa 1960. The evolution of the auto industry is explained using TV monitors and restored automobiles from each period.

Also worth a peek is the permanent "Made in America" exhibit, which traces the evolution of American manufacturing. Far from dull, it explains technology in an entertaining manner, accented by film clips, including one from the *I Love Lucy* show in which Lucy joins a candy-making assembly line with disastrous results. One exhibit, "With Liberty & Justice for All," presents the highlights of four revolutions in America—the American Revolution, the Civil War, the women's suffragist movement, and the Civil Rights era—and features such iconic artifacts as Abraham Lincoln's chair and the bus that Rosa Parks famously rode.

With thousands of items and the adjacent village, the entire complex is more than a bit overwhelming, especially since the museum has an admittedly confusing layout. A good idea is to split a visit into two days, with one day earmarked to explore each half. You might need even more time if you plan to visit other on-site features like the **IMAX Theatre** (show times vary daily, $10-13.75 adults, $9-12.75 seniors

HOMES OF THE AUTO BARONS

As Detroit grew to become the "Motor Capital of the World," opportunities to amass great fortunes grew with it. The automobile "royalty" that emerged took on a pampered lifestyle befitting their status and built great estates full of art and intricate workmanship. Today, these four estates offer visitors the chance to see firsthand how the auto pioneers lived during the heyday of the auto industry.

FISHER MANSION

The only estate within the city limits, the **Fisher Mansion** (383 Lenox Ave., 313/331-6740, www.detroitiskconlive.com), inspired by William Randolph Hearst's San Simeon, was built by Lawrence P. Fisher of the Fisher Body Company, a talented playboy who once courted actress Jean Harlow and who spent millions of his huge fortune constructing this magnificent riverfront estate. It has been described as "glitz bordering on garish." Completed in 1928, it's most noted for its ornate stone and marble work, exquisite European handcrafted stained-glass windows, doors and arches carved from woods imported from India and Africa, and rare black walnut and rosewood parquet floors. More than 200 ounces of gold and silver leaf highlight the decorative ceilings and moldings.

The mansion was neglected after Fisher's death and was initially purchased for just $80,000 in 1975 by Alfred Brush Ford, great-grandson of Henry Ford, and Elisabeth Reuther Dickmeyer, daughter of legendary United Auto Workers chief Walter Reuther. Together, they restored the mansion and donated it to the International Society for Krishna Consciousness, of which they are members. Today, the mansion serves as the Bhaktivedanta Cultural Center, which welcomes the public to daily worship services and special cultural events. Although there are no official tours, visitors to the Fisher Mansion will encounter a fine art gallery and an exhibit about India's colorful heritage.

EDSEL & ELEANOR FORD HOUSE

Where Jefferson Avenue becomes Lake Shore Road stands the **Edsel & Eleanor Ford House** (1100 Lake Shore Rd., Grosse Pointe Shores, 313/884-4222, www.fordhouse.org, house tours 10am-4pm Tues.-Sat., noon-4pm Sun. Apr.-Dec., noon-1:30pm Tues.-Fri., noon-4pm Sat. Jan.-Mar., closed on major holidays and for two weeks in winter, $12 adults, $11 seniors, $8 children 6-12, children under 6 free). The Cotswold-style mansion, designed by noted local architect Albert Kahn, was built in 1929 for Henry Ford's only son, who raised his four children in this house. Much of the interior paneling and furniture was lifted from distinguished old English manors; even the roof is of imported English stones expertly laid by imported Cotswold roofers.

What makes the house especially interesting is that it remains much as it did when the Fords lived there. Edsel died in 1943, but his wife, Eleanor Clay Ford, left the estate virtually untouched after that, meaning that it represents a style of living and quality of craftsmanship that is rapidly vanishing, if not completely gone. Throughout is evidence of the Fords' love of art, with copies of masterpieces now replacing the originals that were donated to the downtown Detroit Institute of Arts.

Visitors can experience a 13-minute video about the Fords, an hour-long guided tour that leads them through the distinctive dwelling, and a self-guided tour of the grounds and outer buildings (9:30am-6pm Tues.-Sat., 11:30am-6pm Sun. Apr.-Dec., 11:30am-4pm Tues.-Sun. Jan.-Mar.). Highlights include a stylish art deco recreation room by famed industrial designer Walter Dorwin Teague; Edsel's personal study, lined with framed family photos and images of luminaries like Thomas Edison; and the Tudor-style playhouse created in 1930 for daughter Josephine's seventh birthday. Note that behind-the-scenes tours ($15 pp, children under 6 free), which include a guided house tour and access to the grounds, are also available. Of course, those who decide not to tour the house can simply meander amid the grounds ($5 pp, children under 6 free).

FAIR LANE

Of the four auto baron estates, Henry Ford's **Fair Lane** (1 Fair Lane Dr., Dearborn, 313/884-4222, www.henryfordestate.org, tours 10:30am-2:30pm Tues.-Sun. Apr.-Dec., 1:30pm Tues.-Sun. Jan.-Mar., $12 adults, $11 seniors and students, $8 children 6-12, children under 6 free) is, surprisingly, the least baronial. By the time it was completed in 1914, Ford had become active in World War I politics and spent a lot of time helping the war effort in Europe. Nonetheless, it is justly listed as a National Historic Landmark.

Fair Lane encompasses more than 1,300 acres. For some, the natural landscape by Jens Jensen is the highlight of a visit; for others, it's the estate's many technical feats, including the extensive six-level hydroelectric power plant created by Ford and his good buddy Thomas Edison. In this house, Ford entertained some of the world's most influential people, including Charles Lindbergh (also a Detroit native), President Herbert Hoover, and the Duke of Windsor. It's an unusual combination of a Scottish baronial structure and the Prairie style developed by Frank Lloyd Wright. Two-hour tours uncover quirky details such as Henry's basement bowling alley and his penchant for birds (he once had 500 birdhouses on the premises) as well as Clara's passion for roses. A small but choice gift shop stocks a wide selection of books on related subjects.

During the summer of 2013, ownership of the historic estate passed to a nonprofit organization that will oversee an extensive restoration. Unfortunately, the property will remain closed to the public during this time.

MEADOW BROOK HALL

Last but not least is Rochester's **Meadow Brook Hall** (480 S. Adams Rd., 248/364-6200, www.oakland.edu/mbh, tours 11:30am-2:30pm daily June-Aug., 1:30pm Mon.-Fri., 11:30am-2:30pm Sat.-Sun. Jan.-May and Sept.-Nov., $15 adults, $10 seniors 62 and over, children under 13 free). John Dodge and his brother Horace were among the car makers responsible for Detroit's sudden catapult into big business. John died suddenly in 1920, leaving behind a vast fortune and a widow, Matilda (his former secretary), who remarried a wealthy lumberman, Alfred Wilson, in 1925. Together, Alfred and Matilda toured Europe and dreamed of a grand estate north of the city. They built the 110-room Tudor-style Meadow Brook Hall in the late 1920s for the then-astonishing sum of $4 million. Interiors were copied from drawings of English estates.

More than 85 years later, Meadow Brook is still largely intact, in part because Mrs. Wilson left the estate to Oakland University, which still administers the property. Rooms — including a two-story ballroom, game rooms copied from old English pubs, and Matilda's bathroom accented with locally made Pewabic tile — still house original family collections and furnishings. A walk in the surrounding woods reveals a six-room playhouse known as Knole Cottage, built for Frances Wilson, Matilda's daughter; typically, the playhouse is open noon-5pm daily during the Holiday Walk (house tours 11am-5pm daily, $20 adults, $5 children 3-17, children under 3 free), an annual celebration that usually takes place late November-December 23. Throughout the year, a behind-the-scenes tour ($15 adults, $10 seniors, children under 13 free), which offers a glimpse at rarely seen parts of the mansion, may also be available.

SOUTHEAST MICHIGAN

The Henry Ford

62 and over, $8.50-9.75 children under 13) and the **Benson Ford Research Center** (9:30am-5pm Tues.-Fri.). In addition, tour buses regularly leave for the **Ford Rouge Factory Tour** (9:30am-5pm Mon.-Sat., $15 adults, $14 seniors 62 and over, $11 children 3-12, children under 3 free), a five-part excursion that culminates with a stroll through the Ford F-150 truck assembly plant.

Accommodations

For those who'd prefer not to stay overnight in downtown Detroit, the city's suburbs offer a number of lodging options, and Dearborn is no exception. **The Dearborn Inn** (20301 Oakwood Blvd., 313/271-2700, www.marriott.com, $139-229 d), for instance, has a terrific location on 23 lush acres. The 229 refined guest rooms and the five Colonial-style guest homes make this a unique hotel experience. Amenities at this smoke-free Marriott property include plush bedding, flat-screen HDTVs, high-speed Internet access, a fitness center, a business center, an on-site restaurant, and an outdoor swimming pool.

Another stylish option is the pet-friendly **Adoba Hotel** (600 Town Center Dr., 313/592-3622, www.adobadearborn.com, $159-199 d), an enormous, postmodern steel-and-glass monolith designed by architect Charles Luckman and housing more than 770 rooms and suites. Not surprisingly, it's one of the largest hotels in the Hyatt chain. The on-site restaurant, Giulio & Sons, serves well-prepared steaks, seafood, and northern Italian specialties. Not far away, **The Henry** (300 Town Center Dr., 313/441-2000, www.behenry.com, $149-259 d), which was built with Ford money, attracts power brokers from across the country as well as a few understated rock stars and visiting celebrities. The award-winning TRIA is known for its excellent, if pricey, continental cuisine, and the elegant rooms feature contemporary artwork, custom furnishings, and free high-speed Internet access. Other on-site amenities include a fitness center, an indoor swimming pool, and massage treatment rooms.

Food
Dearborn offers its share of vittles, too. ❰ **Big Fish** (700 Town Center Dr., 313/336-6350, www.muer.com, 11am-10pm Mon.-Thurs., 11am-11pm Fri., 11:30am-11pm Sat., 1pm-9pm Sun., $10-40), part of the Muer seafood restaurant family, is a popular lunch spot that can also get pretty crowded during dinner. Some say the unusual name is a reference to the Big Three execs who power lunch at the original location in Dearborn (there's also one in Trenton, New Jersey). Others say it's a reference to the menu, which mainly features seafood. The atmosphere is dark and clubby, accented with fishing and nautical motifs. Specialties include the seafood jambalaya, seared diver scallops, steamed Dungeness crab, and any of the excellent daily specials.

Information
For more information about Dearborn, consult the **Dearborn Area Chamber of Commerce** (22100 Michigan Ave., Dearborn, 313/584-6100, www.dearbornchamber.org, 9am-5pm Mon.-Fri.) or the **Detroit Metro Convention & Visitors Bureau** (211 W. Fort St., Ste. 1000, Detroit, 313/202-1800 or 800/338-7648, www.visitdetroit.com, 9am-5pm Mon.-Fri.).

Getting There
Many travelers choose to access Dearborn via train; **Amtrak** (800/872-7245, www.amtrak.com), after all, offers regular service to the town's station at 16121 Michigan Avenue. If, on the other hand, you're driving from downtown Detroit, you can simply take M-10 North and I-94 West to reach Dearborn. Without traffic, this 10-mile trip should take about 15 minutes.

FARMINGTON HILLS
Holocaust Memorial Center
America's first freestanding **Holocaust Memorial Center** (28123 Orchard Lake Rd., 248/553-2400, www.holocaustcenter.org,

9:30am-5pm Sun.-Thurs., 9:30am-3pm Fri., $8 adults, $6 seniors 55 and over, $5-6 students) provides a vivid portrayal of the Holocaust. Features include extensive material and state-of-the-art display techniques that enhance this visceral experience.

Information
For more information about Farmington Hills, consult the **Greater Farmington Area Chamber of Commerce** (33425 Grand River Ave., Ste. 101, Farmington, 248/919-6917, www.gfachamber.com, 9am-5pm Mon.-Fri.) or the **Detroit Metro Convention & Visitors Bureau** (211 W. Fort St., Ste. 1000, Detroit, 313/202-1800 or 800/338-7648, www.visitdetroit.com, 9am-5pm Mon.-Fri.).

Getting There
If you're driving from downtown Detroit, simply take M-10 North, merge onto I-696 West, and follow M-5 East to reach Farmington Hills. Without traffic, this 29-mile trip should take roughly 32 minutes.

ROYAL OAK
Sights and Shopping
Heading north on Woodward from downtown Detroit, Royal Oak is one of the first suburbs you'll encounter after you cross 8 Mile Road. It's the only suburb in the Detroit area where you'll find green hair, unusual pierced body parts, and whips and chains in the window of **Noir Leather** (124 W. 4th St., 248/541-3979, www.noirleather.com, 11am-9pm Mon.-Thurs., 11am-10pm Fri.-Sat., noon-7pm Sun.), a fetish fashion boutique founded in 1983. Nowhere else in Michigan will you find a store sign that reads "Absolutely no return on bondage items for sanitary reasons."

Royal Oak was a sleepy (some said "dying") suburb in the 1970s, known only by its nickname—Royal Joke—and as the site of the respected 125-acre **Detroit Zoo** (8450 W. 10 Mile Rd., 248/541-5717, www.detroitzoo.org, 9am-5pm daily Apr.-Labor Day, 10am-5pm daily Sept.-Oct., 10am-4pm daily Nov.-Mar., $14

SOUTHEAST MICHIGAN

© L. DIGGS OF PICTURE THIS

fountain in Royal Oak's Detroit Zoo

adults, $12 seniors 62 and over, $9 children 2-15, children under 2 free). The zoo, long a popular city attraction, is home to more than 1,300 animals, from flamingos and trumpeter swans to wolverines and gorillas. Three of the most favored exhibits are the Wildlife Interpretive Gallery, site of a popular hummingbird/butterfly garden; the Arctic Ring of Fire, which features polar bears and Arctic species; and the Holden Museum of Living Reptiles.

In the mid-1980s, the city's gay population was concentrated in Royal Oak, filling the two main commercial streets with vintage clothing and record shops, antiques emporiums, and funky coffeehouses. While a few of the original boutiques remain, others have been replaced by high-rent glitzy home furnishings shops and restaurants, which now characterize much of the area. Despite this, Royal Oak is still a lively place, where the streets are filled with a pleasing variety of families and punks, gays and straights. Main Street and Washington Avenue, the two main drags, are great spots for window-shopping and people-watching. And it seems as if a new eatery opens almost every day here, giving it one of the best and most extensive restaurant scenes in metro Detroit.

Worthwhile stops include the sinful **Gayle's Chocolates** (417 S. Washington Ave., 248/398-0001, www.gayleschocolates.com, 10am-6pm Mon.-Wed., 10am-8pm Thurs.-Sat., noon-7pm Sun. fall-spring, 10am-6pm Mon.-Tues., 10am-8pm Wed.-Thurs., 10am-10pm Fri.-Sat., noon-7pm Sun. summer), the first in the city to offer cappuccino and espresso (now found on just about every corner). Another feature is the popular juice bar (try the carrot-apple-ginger), but Gayle's heart remains in the chocolate-making facility located upstairs, which churns out some of the best truffles in the country. Also worth a peek are **Vertu** (514 S. Washington Ave., 248/545-6050, www.vertumodern.com, noon-6pm Tues.-Sat.), known for its 20th-century designs, including furniture by Charles and Ray Eames, George Nelson, and Eero Saarinen, and **Dos Manos** (210 W. 6th St., 248/542-5856 or 800/572-4957, www.dosmanos.com, 10am-6pm daily), where you'll find Latin American handicrafts.

Food

When it's time to eat in Royal Oak, you'll be hard-pressed to choose. In the mood for seafood? If so, head to **Tom's Oyster Bar** (318 S. Main St., 248/541-1186, www.tomsoysterbar.com, 11am-10pm Mon.-Tues., 11am-11pm Wed.-Thurs., 11am-midnight Fri., noon-1am Sat., noon-10pm Sun., $8-40), which features the area's most extensive selection of—surprise!—oysters, as well as tasty steaks and innovative fresh seafood. **BD's Mongolian Barbecue** (430 S. Main St., 248/398-7755, www.gomongo.com, 11am-10pm Sun.-Fri., 11am-11pm Sat., $6-21), meanwhile, lets you watch as chefs whip up your stir-fry creation on a huge, central grill. Since its opening in 1992, it's become so popular that it has established outposts in other metro Detroit suburbs, not to mention various U.S. states, from Illinois to Florida.

Information

For more information about Royal Oak, consult the **Royal Oak Downtown Development Authority** (211 Williams St., Royal Oak, 248/246-3280, www.downtownroyaloak.org) or the **Detroit Metro Convention & Visitors Bureau** (211 W. Fort St., Ste. 1000, Detroit, 313/202-1800 or 800/338-7648, www.visitdetroit.com, 9am-5pm Mon.-Fri.).

Getting There

Some travelers may choose to access Royal Oak via **Amtrak** (800/872-7245, www.amtrak.com), which offers train service to the sheltered platform at 202 South Sherman Drive. If, on the other hand, you opt to drive from downtown Detroit, simply take I-75 North and Woodward Avenue to reach Royal Oak. Without traffic, this 14-mile trip should take less than 30 minutes.

BIRMINGHAM

Naysayers were concerned that downtown Birmingham—a chic enclave of expensive shops and galleries—would shrivel and die when the even more chic Somerset Collection, a gleaming shopping complex, opened on nearby West Big Beaver Road late in 1996. Birmingham has proven remarkably resilient, however, and remains a tony 'burb with one of the few thriving downtown areas in surrounding Oakland County. Shoppers from all over the metro area come here to see and be seen, to linger in cafés and restaurants, and to exercise their credit cards in the unusual boutiques.

Shopping

Even if you're not a shopper, Birmingham is worth a trip for its art galleries, one of the most impressive concentrations in the Midwest. Here, you'll even find cutting-edge contemporary art at places like the **Robert Kidd Gallery** (107 Townsend St., 248/642-3909, www.robertkiddgallery.com, 11am-5:30pm Tues.-Sat.), which has been in existence since 1976. More than a dozen influential art outlets are grouped along a section of Woodward north of downtown known as "Gallery Row."

Accommodations

In Birmingham, **⟨ The Townsend Hotel** (100 Townsend St., 248/642-7900, www.townsendhotel.com, $250-300 d) is the posh—if relatively unpretentious—European-style hostelry where Paul McCartney stayed when he performed in Detroit in 2005. Nothing but the best is good enough here—Belgian linens, pillows of the fluffiest down, yards of marble in the baths, and a restaurant staffed with world-class chefs who cater to the guests' every whim. You'll feel as if you've stepped into a Ralph Lauren ad. Located near Birmingham's fashionable shops and galleries, it's also a favorite stop for afternoon tea, served every afternoon.

Information

For more information about Birmingham, consult the **Birmingham Principal Shopping District** (151 Martin St., Birmingham, 248/530-1200, www.enjoybirmingham.com) or the **Detroit Metro Convention & Visitors Bureau** (211 W. Fort St., Ste. 1000, Detroit, 313/202-1800 or 800/338-7648, www.visitdetroit.com, 9am-5pm Mon.-Fri.).

Getting There

Some travelers may choose to access Birmingham via **Amtrak** (800/872-7245, www.amtrak.com), which offers train service to the sheltered platform at Villa Road and Lewis Street. If, on the other hand, you opt to drive from downtown Detroit, simply take I-75 North and Woodward Avenue to reach Birmingham. Without traffic, this 20-mile trip should take about 30 minutes.

BLOOMFIELD HILLS

For a look at how the other half (actually, the other 1 percent) lives, turn the wheel north to Bloomfield Hills. Long the suburb of choice for CEOs, Big Three bigwigs, and other members of the city's power brokers, it ranks as the state's richest town as well as the second-wealthiest in the country. Past and present residents have included Detroit Pistons captain Isaiah Thomas and the queen of soul, Aretha Franklin. Unlike Grosse Pointe, which still struggles with the remains of its WASPish heritage, it doesn't matter if you're black or white in Bloomfield Hills. Money is the great equalizer.

If Grosse Pointe epitomizes "old money," Bloomfield Hills attracts its newer, shinier counterpart. Huge houses are spread throughout its rolling hills—a geographic anomaly in southeastern Michigan. Most are late 20th century, although older models can be found clustered around Cranbrook, former home of newspaper magnate George Booth, who founded the *Detroit News*. Drive the winding lanes and you'll find Old Tudor, Georgian, and other 1920s-era mansions. One notable exception is the "Smith House" at 5045 Pon Valley Road, which was designed by Frank Lloyd Wright in 1946.

Cranbrook

Despite its celebrities, Bloomfield Hills remains best known as home to **Cranbrook** (39221 N. Woodward Ave., 877/462-7262, www.cranbrook.edu), a renowned, 315-acre arts and educational complex. Here, famed Finnish architect Eliel Saarinen created a lush and lovely refuge for artists and students.

Cranbrook is known throughout the world for the integrated aesthetics of its environment. All buildings, gardens, sculpture, and interiors are treated as an integral and important part of a whole. This creative cohesion is the result of two men, patron newspaper magnate George Booth and artist Eliel Saarinen. Booth, one of the early city expatriates, bought a rundown farm in Bloomfield Hills in 1904 and commissioned noted Detroit architect Albert Kahn to build him a large, Tudor-style mansion there. Grandson of an English coppersmith, Booth was a noted proponent of the arts-and-crafts movement, which preached a reunification of life and art. After a 1922 trip to Rome, where he visited the American Academy, he decided to create a school of architecture and design.

While the school is still known throughout the world, equal acclaim is drawn by the **Cranbrook Art Museum** (248/645-3323, www.cranbrookartmuseum.org, 11am-5pm

Cranbrook Art Museum

© L. DIGGS OF PICTURE THIS...

Wed.-Sun. June-Aug., 10am-5pm Tues.-Fri., 11am-5pm Sat.-Sun. Sept.-May, $8 adults, $6 seniors 65 and over, $4 students, children under 13 free), which is operated by the **Cranbrook Academy of Art** (248/645-3300, www.cran-brookart.edu) and serves as the largest museum in southeastern Michigan devoted to modern and contemporary art, architecture, and design. It presents exhibits by both students as well as prominent faculty members. Another popular attraction here is the **Cranbrook Institute of Science** (248/645-3200 or 877/462-7262, http://science.cranbrook.edu, 10am-5pm Tues.-Thurs., 10am-10pm Fri.-Sat., noon-4pm Sun., $13 adults, $9.50 seniors 65 and over and children 2-12, children under 2 free), a family-friendly science and natural history museum with a collection of more than 200,000 objects and artifacts. In addition to galleries devoted to geology, anthropology, astronomy, Native Americans, and other riveting subjects, popular diversions here include a planetarium ($5 pp, $1 children under 2), a live bat program ($5 pp, $1 children under 2), and an observatory that's open (and free) to the public on Friday and Saturday evenings, weather permitting.

Accommodations

If you're hoping to stay overnight in Bloomfield Hills, head to the **Radisson Hotel Detroit-Bloomfield Hills** (39475 Woodward Ave., 248/644-1400, www.radisson.com, $110-160 d), a comfortable property in a prime location. In addition to more than 150 rooms and suites, the Radisson offers a fitness center, an indoor heated pool, a business center, three on-site dining options, free high-speed Internet access, and shuttle service within a 10-mile radius.

Information

For more information about Bloomfield Hills, consult the **City of Bloomfield Hills** (45 E. Long Lake Rd., Bloomfield Hills, 248/644-1520, www.bloomfieldhillsmi.net) or the **Detroit Metro Convention & Visitors Bureau** (211 W. Fort St., Ste. 1000, Detroit, 313/202-1800 or 800/338-7648, www.visitdetroit.com, 9am-5pm Mon.-Fri.).

Getting There

If you're driving from downtown Detroit, take M-10 North and US-24 North to reach Bloomfield Hills. Without traffic, this 26-mile trip should take roughly 30 minutes.

GROSSE POINTE

Five cities actually make up the area collectively known as Grosse Pointe on Detroit's far east side. Taken as a whole, Grosse Pointe Shores, Grosse Pointe Farms, Grosse Pointe Woods, the city of Grosse Pointe, and Grosse Pointe Park make up one of the metro area's wealthiest suburbs, a land of landscaped estates, big trees, big homes, and even bigger money.

A summer community in the 1840s, Grosse Pointe began to change about 1910, when wealthy Detroiters sought to separate themselves from the immigrants who crowded the growing city. The wealthiest built mansions that imitated the elegant country houses of England, France, and Italy, importing stone fireplaces and entire rooms that were later incorporated into new construction.

This is where the city's prominent old families settled; many descendants of this founding aristocracy still live here. For years (through roughly the 1950s), prospective home buyers were screened by a Grosse Pointe real estate broker's infamous point system designed to perpetuate WASP homogeneity. Today, you'll find a much more diverse population, although, like most of Detroit's suburbs, it's still predominantly white. Grosse Pointe Park is the most liberal and Democratic, with a number of smaller homes and modest, middle-class 1920s housing. One area, now known as the Cabbage Patch because its early Belgian residents grew the vegetable in their yards, was developed to house servants from the nearby estates.

Sights

Many of the largest mansions have been razed, although a few remain along Lake Shore Drive. It's a beautiful drive in any season, with the Detroit River attracting joggers, freighter-watchers, and others who come just to ogle the architecture. To get a peek at the inside of one of the area's original estates, stop at the former **Alger House,** now known as the **Grosse Pointe War Memorial** (32 Lake Shore Dr., Grosse Pointe Farms, 313/881-7511, www.warmemorial.org, 9am-9pm Mon.-Sat., free). Built in 1910, this roomy Italian Renaissance-style mansion was originally the home of a founder of the Packard Motor Company and now serves as a community center.

Information

For more information about Grosse Pointe, consult the **Grosse Pointe Chamber of** **Commerce** (63 Kercheval Ave., Ste. 16, Grosse Pointe, 313/881-4722, www.grossepointecham-ber.com, 9am-5pm Mon.-Fri.) or the **Detroit Metro Convention & Visitors Bureau** (211 W. Fort St., Ste. 1000, Detroit, 313/202-1800 or 800/338-7648, www.visitdetroit.com, 9am-5pm Mon.-Fri.).

Getting There

If you're driving from downtown Detroit, take East Jefferson Avenue to reach Grosse Pointe. Without traffic, this eight-mile trip should take about 20 minutes.

Southeast Michigan

In the towns surrounding the Detroit metropolitan area, visitors will find nostalgic downtown districts, historic museums, inland lakes, and recreation areas galore—all a relatively quick drive from Detroit via interstates and major highways.

GROSSE ILE

Not far from the Detroit River International Wildlife Refuge, Grosse Ile is a lengthy, bottle-shaped island in the Detroit River, just north of the entrance to Lake Erie.

Sights

LIGHTHOUSES

While Grosse Ile isn't a huge tourist destination, there are two nearby lighthouses worth a look: the **Grosse Ile North Channel Range Front Light,** a white, 50-foot-tall octagonal tower lit in 1906 and deactivated in 1963, and the **Detroit River Light** in Lake Erie, only accessible via boat. Although the **Grosse Ile Historical Society** (P.O. Box 131, Grosse Ile, MI 48138, 734/675-1250, www.gihistory.org) offers an annual one-day tour of the Grosse Ile lighthouse, the Detroit River Light, which was built in 1885 and is still an active navigational aid operated by the U.S. Coast Guard, can only be viewed from the outside. Curiously, the Detroit River Light has also been known as the Bar Point Shoal Light.

⟨ LAKE ERIE METROPARK

Perhaps surprising to some, southeastern Michigan boasts several parks and natural areas, ideal for outdoor enthusiasts weary of Detroit's downtown bustle. Perhaps even more surprising, the Detroit area is the site of North America's first international wildlife refuge. Established in 2001, the **Detroit River International Wildlife Refuge** (Brownstown Charter Township, 734/365-0219, www.fws. gov/midwest/detroitriver) comprises islands, marshes, coastal wetlands, and waterfront terrain along the lower Detroit River and western shoreline of Lake Erie. Though public access is limited, you can appreciate at least part of the refuge by visiting the **Lake Erie Metropark** (32481 W. Jefferson, Brownstown, 734/379-5020, www.metroparks.com, 6am-10pm daily in summer, 7am-8pm daily in winter, $7/vehicle daily, $20-30/vehicle annually), a well-preserved, 1,607-acre recreation area situated south of Grosse Ile and offering stunning views of the nearby river, lake, and islands. Popular among outdoor enthusiasts, the metropark features three miles of shoreline, an 18-hole golf course (734/379-0048), hiking and biking trails, a swimming pool, a marina and boat launches (7am-9pm daily Memorial Day-Labor Day, $7 daily, $20-35 annually), and the **Marshlands Museum and Nature Center** (9am-5pm daily in summer, 1pm-5pm Mon.-Fri., 9am-5pm Sat.-Sun. in winter, free with admission to the park). While anglers, kayakers, and bird-watchers enjoy this peaceful place in the spring, summer, and fall, the Lake Erie Metropark is also favored during the winter months, when cross-country skiers can enjoy 4.25 miles of flat, groomed trails.

Food

If you're hungry after visiting Grosse Ile, return to the mainland and grab a bite to eat. One tasty option is the **Speedboat Bar & Grill** (749 Biddle Ave., Wyandotte, 734/282-5750, www.speedboatbar-grill.com, 11am-10pm Tues.-Thurs., 10am-2am Fri., 11am-2am Sat., $4-17), home of the masterpiece swine burger, maybe the perfect bar burger. It's thick and juicy and served with spicy rings of jalapeño, pepper cheese, chili, and fried onions. Or you can opt for a brimming bowl of the spicy red chili, a consistent award-winner. This joint is definitely worth a special trip downriver.

Information

For more information about Grosse Ile, consult the **Township of Grosse Ile** (9601 Groh Rd., Grosse Ile, 734/676-4422, www.grosseile.com, 8am-5pm Mon.-Fri.).

Getting There

To reach Grosse Ile Township from downtown Detroit, take M-10 North and I-75 South to West Road East, turn right onto Allen Road, turn left onto Van Horn Road, take another left onto West Jefferson Avenue, and then take an immediate right onto Grosse Ile Parkway, which connects the mainland to Grosse Ile. Without traffic, this 27-mile trip should take about 40 minutes.

MONROE

On the banks of the River Raisin, in Michigan's southeastern corner, lies the city of Monroe, Michigan's third-oldest community. Its location made it the natural crossroads for the Native Americans, the French missionaries, and the fur trappers who settled in the area. Caught between the British Army and the U.S. forces during the War of 1812, Monroe is also the site of the deadliest battle during the war, when after having been pushed back into Canada, the British counterattacked, killing 300 Americans in the Battle of the River Raisin. "Remember the Raisin" became America's rally cry after the Indian allies of the British killed another hundred injured soldiers who were unable to retreat after the battle. In the 19th century, Monroe also became home to General George A. Custer and his wife, Elizabeth.

Sights and Shopping

History buffs might enjoy a visit to the **Monroe County Historical Museum** (126 S. Monroe St., 734/240-7780, www.co.monroe.mi.us/museum, by appt. Mon.-Tues., 10am-5pm Wed.-Sat., noon-5pm Sun., $4 adults, $2 children 5-17, children under 5 free), a Georgian-style public building that houses one of the largest collections of 18th- and 19th-century artifacts relating to southeastern Michigan. Of course, with shopping and dining possibilities galore, this quaint town offers more than just history. Check out the year-round **Monroe Farmers Market** (17 E. Willow St., www.farmersmarketmonroe.com, 6am-noon Tues. and Sat. June-Oct., 7am-1pm Sat. Nov.-May) for some locally produced treats.

To better enjoy the riverfront, you can purchase an inexpensive bike from **Jack's Bicycles** (206 S. Monroe St., 734/242-1400, www.jacksbike.com, 10am-6pm Mon.-Fri., 10am-4pm Sat.), a fantastic shop with a huge variety of bikes, plus sporty apparel. If you want to splurge on yourself or someone else, check out **Frenchie's** (15 E. Front St., 734/242-5840, www.frenchiesjewelry.com, 10am-5pm Mon.-Fri., 10am-3pm Sat.), where you can browse through their extensive coin, stamp, and fine jewelry collections.

Information

For more information about Monroe, contact the **Monroe County Convention and Tourism Bureau** (103 W. Front St., 734/457-1030, www.monroeinfo.com, 10am-6pm Tues.-Fri., 9am-4pm Sat.) or the **Monroe County Chamber of Commerce** (P.O. Box 626, Monroe, MI 48161, 734/384-3366, www.monroecountychamber.com, 8:30am-5pm Mon.-Fri.).

Getting There

From downtown Detroit via car, take I-75 South to Monroe. Without traffic, this 40-mile trip should take about 40 minutes.

PONTIAC

In its heyday, Pontiac was a booming General Motors town. While still the home of several manufacturing plants, it's clear that Pontiac has seen better days. Nevertheless, the town still has a lot to offer for visitors and residents alike.

Sights

Perched on 4.5 acres of well-groomed land and home to the Oakland County Pioneer and Historical Society, the **Pine Grove Historical Museum** (405 Cesar Chavez Ave., 248/338-6732, www.ocphs.org, 11am-4pm Tues.-Thurs., $5 adults, $3 children under 13) comprises what was once known as Pine Grove, the former estate of Moses Wisner, one of Michigan's pre-Civil War governors. Today, it encompasses the Wisner Mansion and several outbuildings, including a summer kitchen, an outhouse, a smokehouse, and a root cellar. On the premises, you'll also encounter the Drayton Plains one-room schoolhouse and a carriage house that's home to a research library as well as the Pioneer Museum. The collections here include classic automobiles, 19th-century tools and farming implements, and vintage clothing from the 19th and early 20th centuries, including military uniforms from the Civil War, the Spanish-American War, World War I, and World War II.

Entertainment and Events

NIGHTLIFE

Surprisingly, Pontiac has a thriving club scene, boasting some of southeastern Michigan's hippest joints. **Clutch Cargo's** (65 E. Huron, 248/333-2362 or 248/333-0649, www.clutchcargos.com, show times and ticket prices vary) is a nightclub and music venue that regularly books big-name talent. The **Tonic Night Club** (29 S. Saginaw St., 248/334-7411, www.tonicdetroit.com, 10pm-2am Thurs., 9pm-2am Fri.-Sun., cover varies), meanwhile, offers multiple dance floors and some of Detroit's hottest DJs; over the years, it's welcomed a plethora of celebrities, from Prince to Justin Timberlake.

◖ WOODWARD DREAM CRUISE

Begun in 1995 as a small fundraiser for the Ferndale community, this annual mid-August parade down Woodward Avenue has become the world's largest one-day automotive event, luring 1.5 million people and more than 40,000 classic cars from around the globe. The **Woodward Dream Cruise** (www.woodwarddreamcruise.com) stretches 16 miles though Ferndale, Pleasant Ridge, Huntington Woods, Berkley, Royal Oak, Birmingham, Bloomfield Hills, Bloomfield Township, and Pontiac, taking over Woodward Avenue through each of these towns—truly a spectacle to behold. Luckily, it's free to watch, but find your spot early, as it gets very crowded all along the route.

Sports and Recreation

GOLF

While golfers will find the largest concentration of well-regarded golf courses in the northern half of the Lower Peninsula, southeastern Michigan has a few notable spots as well. One such option is **Shepherd's Hollow Golf Club** (9085 Big Lake Rd., Clarkston, 248/922-0300, www.shepherdshollow.com, daily Apr.-Oct., $40-75 pp w/cart). Situated northwest of Pontiac and Waterford, this scenic championship course offers 27 holes amid 350 acres of rolling, wooded terrain.

Information

For more information about Pontiac, consult the **City of Pontiac** (47450 Woodward Ave., 248/758-3000, www.pontiac.mi.us).

Getting There

Some travelers reach Pontiac via **Amtrak** (800/872-7245, www.amtrak.com) or **Greyhound** (248/333-2499 or 800/231-2222, www.greyhound.com), which offer regular train and bus service, respectively, to the station building at 51000 Woodward Avenue. If, on the other hand, you're driving from downtown Detroit, take I-375 North, merge onto I-75 North, and follow the I-75 Business Loop to Woodward Avenue, which will lead you to Pontiac. Without traffic, this 31-mile trip should take about 35 minutes.

AUBURN HILLS

Shopping

In recent years, the Detroit area has seen an influx of outlet malls. One of the biggest and best is located in Auburn Hills.

The **Great Lakes Crossing Outlets** (4000 Baldwin Rd., 877/746-7452, www.shopgreatlakescrossingoutlets.com, 10am-9pm Mon.-Sat., 11am-6pm Sun., holiday hours vary) has almost 200 stores and restaurants. With everything from Brooks Brothers to Nike, the mall is sure to satisfy your shopping fix. Even movie lovers will be happy here; there's an enormous AMC multiplex on-site. If you're visiting during the holiday season, plan for huge crowds and long walks from your parking spot.

Information

For more information about Auburn Hills, contact the **Auburn Hills Chamber of Commerce** (3395A Auburn Rd., 248/853-7862, www.auburnhillschamber.com, 9am-4pm Mon.-Thurs., 9am-1pm Fri.).

Getting There

From downtown Detroit via car, take I-375 North, I-75 North, and Lapeer Road to reach Auburn Hills. Without traffic, this 33-mile trip should take about 35 minutes.

ANN ARBOR AND THE HEARTLAND

From any point in the Great Lakes State, at least one of the five Great Lakes (all but Lake Ontario) is never more than 90 miles away. That's auspicious news for Michigan's Heartland—also known as Central Michigan—the only region that doesn't sit astride the coast. Stretching from the southern state line to the middle of the Lower Peninsula, this wide swath of rolling prairies, scenic lakes, weathered barns, and abundant farmland contains some of the state's finest educational institutions and largest cities, including Grand Rapids, Kalamazoo, Midland, and Lansing, the state capital since 1847.

As with the Thumb, travelers often overlook Michigan's Heartland. Early settlers of the 19th century, however, recognized the appeal of this centralized region. A surge of eager, frontier-bound settlers resulted in the creation of some of Michigan's most picturesque towns, including Marshall, which has been designated a National Historic Landmark District for its varied 19th-century architecture. Migrating Easterners were also responsible for the establishment of many of the Heartland's private colleges, in towns such as Hillsdale, Albion, Alma, and Olivet. A hotbed of academia, the Heartland also has its share of major universities—most notably, the University of Michigan in Ann Arbor, with other standouts nearby, including Western Michigan University in Kalamazoo, Michigan State University in East Lansing, and Central Michigan University in Mount Pleasant.

Besides strolling through the well-groomed campuses and well-preserved villages that

HIGHLIGHTS

© AVALON TRAVEL

❰❰ Bird-Watching Near Augusta: The W. K. Kellogg Bird Sanctuary is one of America's pioneer wildlife conservation centers. Hike amid 180 acres of diverse habitats, which nurture hundreds of bird species (page 76).

❰❰ Air Zoo: Devoted to aviation and space exploration, this enormous complex invites visitors to explore an incredible assortment of interactive exhibits and historic displays, including flight simulators, World War II-era bombers, astronaut artifacts, and a pseudo-paratrooper jump (page 82).

❰❰ Gerald R. Ford Presidential Museum: In addition to celebrating the lives of President Ford and his wife, the museum offers temporary exhibits from the Smithsonian Institution and the National Archives (page 85).

❰❰ Frederik Meijer Gardens and Sculpture Park: This impressive collection of gardens also boasts a tropical conservatory as well as sculptures by Auguste Rodin, Claes Oldenburg, and Henry Moore (page 87).

❰❰ Michigan State University: Stroll through several lovely gardens, attend Big 10 football games, view an assortment of art and science exhibits, and catch a wide array of live performances at the Wharton Center (page 91).

❰❰ University of Michigan: Even if you're not a U of M student, you can still appreciate the school's wide array of diversions, including museums, art galleries, gardens, live theaters, and, of course, football (page 58).

❰❰ Purple Rose Theatre Company: Founded by award-winning actor Jeff Daniels, this Chelsea-based playhouse was named in honor of the Woody Allen film *The Purple Rose of Cairo* (1985). Audiences travel far and wide to catch the latest play at this renowned theater (page 66).

❰❰ Marshall's Historic Homes: Picturesque Marshall contains over 850 19th-century homes and businesses, in a variety of architectural styles. In 1991, the town was designated a National Historic Landmark District (page 72).

❰❰ Soaring Eagle Casino and Resort: One of the Midwest's largest casinos offers thousands of slot machines and table games, several restaurants, over 500 luxurious rooms, a soothing spa, and live entertainment (page 98).

❰❰ Saginaw Chippewa Tribal Powwow: In early August, the Saginaw Chippewa Indian Tribe hosts a gathering of the clans that showcases traditional dancing, drumming, chanting, and cuisine (page 98).

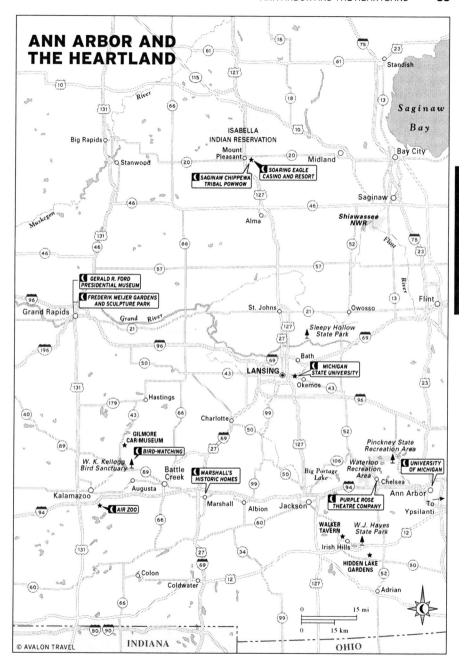

ANN ARBOR AND THE HEARTLAND

THE HEARTLAND

comprise Michigan's Heartland, travelers will find a myriad of other outdoor and cultural pursuits here as well. Whether exploring the Gerald R. Ford Presidential Museum, marveling at Kalamazoo's Air Zoo, hiking through the W. K. Kellogg Bird Sanctuary, or watching a show at the Purple Rose Theatre Company (established by Chelsea native and Hollywood actor Jeff Daniels), coast-conscious visitors will be grateful for the inland detour.

PLANNING YOUR TIME

Michigan's Heartland is an enormous place, extending from the Indiana border to M-20, near the center of the Lower Peninsula; it's bordered on the eastern side by Ann Arbor and Midland, and on the western side by Kalamazoo and Grand Rapids. Given its size, what you're able to see depends on your schedule; likewise, your interests will determine how long you plan to linger in the Heartland. If you only intend to visit the area's major cities, like Lansing and Battle Creek, you should put aside about 5 days. You'll need at least 10 days, however, if you also want to explore the region's outdoor attractions and smaller towns like Chelsea, Marshall, and Mount Pleasant.

Reaching the Heartland is easy. Given the presence of several major towns and cities, it's possible to get here by plane, train, or bus. The region has several commercial airports, in or near places like Kalamazoo, Grand Rapids, Lansing, Midland, and nearby Flint and Detroit. Amtrak and Greyhound both offer routes to Kalamazoo, Battle Creek, East Lansing, Jackson, Ann Arbor, and Grand Rapids. Needless to say, though, the Heartland is not a compact region, so, despite the presence of several public transit systems, having a car is a must—whether you bring your own or rent one in an airport. Major highways and interstates—such as US-23, US-127, US-131, I-69, I-75, I-94, and I-96—make it a snap to get from one end of the Heartland to the other—if you have the time.

The good news is that, save for the Heartland's major museums, annual festivals, and college football games, this centralized region isn't as much of a draw for tourists as coastal locales like Saugatuck, Holland, and Traverse City. So, crowds are often less of a problem here—unless, of course, you simply hate big cities in general.

For more information about Michigan's Heartland, consult **Travel Michigan** (Michigan Economic Development Corporation, 300 N. Washington Sq., Lansing, 888/784-7328, www.michigan.org) or the **West Michigan Tourist Association** (WMTA, 741 Kenmoor Ave., Ste. E, Grand Rapids, 616/245-2217, www.wmta.org).

HISTORY

By the 1830s, Michigan fever had become an epidemic. Pioneer families from all over the East Coast headed west via the newly completed Erie Canal, passed through Detroit, and continued along the new Detroit-Chicago Road, which cut across the southern half of the state's Lower Peninsula. Their final destination: Michigan's rolling prairies, with rich soil and fertile land that the federal government was selling for the bargain-basement price of $1.25 an acre.

Many of the early settlers were Easterners, leaving already-overwhelming cities to seek better opportunities for themselves and their families. The onrush between 1825 and 1855 spurred the settlement of some of Michigan's largest towns, including Battle Creek and Jackson. That early growth was soon augmented by the railroad; by 1849, Michigan Central began making regular state crossings, disgorging thousands of optimistic settlers along the way.

In the region known as Michigan's Heartland, the most visible evidence of these early settlers can be found in the Greek Revival homes and clean-lined architecture of the cities and villages they built. They also founded a number of Eastern-style private colleges, a concentration unmatched elsewhere in the state.

Ann Arbor and Vicinity

Few would dispute the claim that Ann Arbor, with its population of roughly 116,100, is one of the most interesting cities in the state—if not the country. Home to the well-reputed University of Michigan, part of the Big Ten Conference, it transcends the typical college-town atmosphere with its unique blend of large-city verve and small-town friendliness. Located about 40 miles west of Detroit, Ann Arbor is now a regional research center as well as the

suburb of choice for Detroit intelligentsia. Popular with all demographic groups, the city has been awarded the title "Quintessentially Cool College Town" by *Seventeen*, rated the second most "Woman Friendly City in America" by *Ladies Home Journal*, and ranked #46 on *Money* magazine's 2010 list of the "Best Places to Live" in America.

The media continues to heap accolades on the city, in part because of its appealing blend

THE HEARTLAND

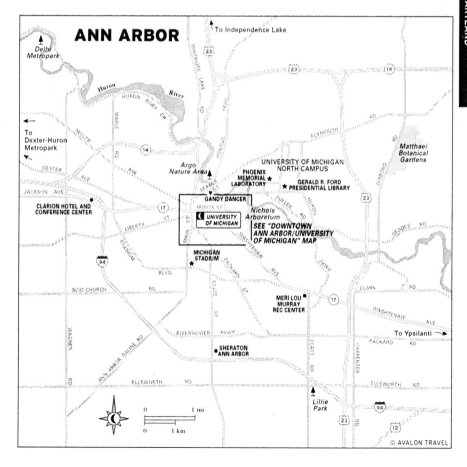

of big-city vitality and small-town Midwestern friendliness. This is Michigan, after all. While there's plenty of typical college-town angst, folks are genuinely helpful when you ask for directions and are always ready to recommend a favorite restaurant.

The city is dominated by the well-known university, which occupies most of the area just east of downtown. Historic U of M, founded in 1817, is one of the nation's great public institutions, with a long reputation for excellence in academics and athletics. The university is proud of its statistics, including having the largest pre-law and pre-med programs in the country; graduates that include eight NASA astronauts, one president, numerous actors and filmmakers, and several Pulitzer Prize and Nobel Prize winners; and a diverse student body that represents all 50 states and more than 100 foreign countries.

SIGHTS
◖ University of Michigan

A campus tour of the **University of Michigan** (www.umich.edu) reveals the expected and the less expected—both backpacked and Birkenstocked students and a quirky collection of 2,500 rare musical instruments. The heart of it all is the **"Diag,"** the diagonal walkway crossing the original 40-acre campus between State Street, North University, and South University. Many of the buildings house classrooms, and on many days this is the site of student protest demonstrations and outdoor concerts. Ann Arbor, while still politically aware these days, is not the hotbed of activism it was in the 1960s, when an ongoing campaign began here to legalize marijuana.

For a terrific view, climb the eight floors to the map room in the **Harlan Hatcher Graduate Library.** Afterward, cross State Street, where you'll find the venerable **Michigan Union** (530 S. State St., 734/763-5750, 7am-2am Mon.-Sat., 9am-2am Sun. fall/winter, 7am-midnight Mon.-Thurs., 7am-2am Fri.-Sat., 9am-midnight Sun. spring/summer), built in the 1920s and site of President Kennedy's announcement to form the Peace Corps. Just

north of the Diag, you'll find another historic student union, the **Michigan League** (911 N. University Ave., 734/764-0446, 7am-11pm daily), opened in 1929 as a center for women's social and cultural activities on campus; today, it houses a gift shop, an information center, a 640-seat theater, and a small inn for visitors.

Across from the League is the **Burton Memorial Tower,** a campus landmark that's capped by one of the world's heaviest carillons, containing 43 tons of bells. Another campus favorite is the **Law Quadrangle,** home of U of M's respected law school. Built 1923-1933, the picturesque quad was modeled after Britain's Cambridge University. The level of workmanship in the Gothic building was rare even in the arts-and-crafts inspired 1920s. Rest your feet in the library's hushed reading room, where maize and blue plaster medallions decorate the ceiling.

No visit to Wolverine territory would be complete without a stop at **Michigan Stadium** on Stadium Street and Main. The largest collegiate stadium in the United States, it draws more than 105,000 screaming fans for home games and post-game tailgating marathons. Constructed in 1927, this historic stadium has remained open and active ever since, even through a massive, much-needed renovation that was completed in 2010.

Campus Museums

Established in 1817, U of M has long been a leading research institution; over the years, it's developed extensive collections. Most are housed in the university's exceptional museums. The **University of Michigan Museum of Natural History** (1109 Geddes Ave., 734/764-0480, www.lsa.umich.edu/ummnh, 9am-5pm Mon.-Sat., noon-5pm Sun., donation suggested) is one of the best natural science museums in the country, with displays on prehistoric life, dinosaurs, anthropology, Native Americans, Michigan wildlife, and geology. Most of the highlights—especially the dinosaur dioramas—are on the 2nd floor.

Among the top 10 U.S. university art museums, the **University of Michigan Museum**

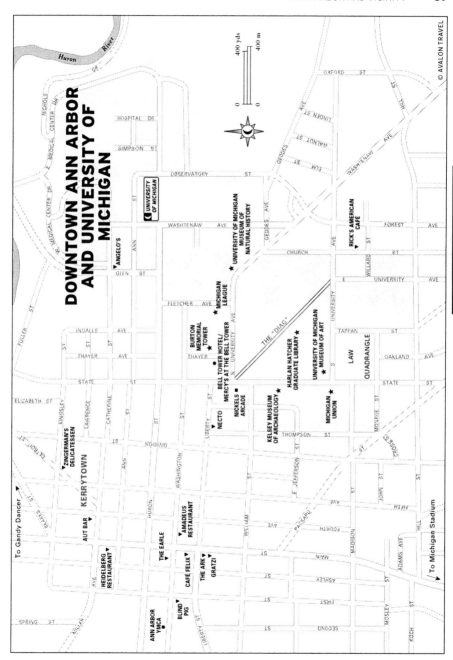

DOWNTOWN ANN ARBOR AND UNIVERSITY OF MICHIGAN

© AVALON TRAVEL

THE HEARTLAND

THE HEARTLAND

© 123RF.COM

University of Michigan

of Art (525 S. State St., 734/764-0395, www. umma.umich.edu, 10am-5pm Tues.-Sat., noon-5pm Sun., free though $5 donation suggested) has a permanent collection of more than 15,000 regularly rotated pieces, including works by big names like Picasso, Miró, Cézanne, and more. Masterpieces include Max Beckmann's *Begin the Beguine,* Monet's *The Break-up of the Ice,* and the especially strong collection of Whistler prints. The knowledgeable staff works hard to make art more accessible and relevant to the general public, with a high-caliber museum shop, enthusiastic docents, and a weekly series of gallery talks, art videos, and slide lectures. In March 2009, the museum completed a massive renovation of its historic home, Alumni Memorial Hall, and unveiled a 53,000-square-foot expansion dedicated to its lead benefactors, Maxine and Stuart Frankel.

Other intriguing museums include the **Gerald R. Ford Presidential Library** (1000 Beal Ave., 734/205-0555, www.ford.utexas. edu, 8:45am-4:45pm Mon.-Fri., free), an enormous collection of letters, reports, photographs,

televised campaign commercials, audiotapes of speeches, and other archival materials, and the **Sindecuse Museum of Dentistry** (Kellogg Building, 1011 N. University Ave., www.dent. umich.edu, 8am-6pm Mon.-Fri., free), a rare collection of over 10,000 objects focused on the history of dentistry from the 18th century to the present. In addition, the **Stearns Collection of Musical Instruments** (1100 Baits Dr., 734/764-0583, www.music.umich. edu, 10am-5pm Mon.-Fri., free) is a fascinatingly quirky repository of over 2,500 musical instruments collected by drug manufacturer Fred Stearns. The collection features permanent and occasional displays throughout the Earl V. Moore Building of the School of Music, Theatre & Dance in the North Campus area.

University Gardens

If you enjoy perusing collections of a more natural kind, then take some time to stroll through the University of Michigan's lovely gardens. The **Matthaei Botanical Gardens** (1800 N. Dixboro Rd., 734/647-7600, www.

lsa.umich.edu/mbg, grounds 8am-sunset daily, conservatory 10am-4:30pm Tues. and Thurs.-Sun., 10am-8pm Wed., $5 adults, $2 students, grounds free) is an ideal place for a nature walk. In addition to an expansive conservatory of tropical, warm-temperate, and desert plants, you'll find picturesque gardens, several nature trails, and a re-created prairie.

The **Nichols Arboretum** (1610 Washington Heights Rd., 734/647-7600, www.lsa.umich.edu/mbg, 8am-sunset daily, free) offers some of the area's best hiking trails and a natural area that serves as an education and research facility for the university. It's located next to the central campus and offers more than 400 identified tree species, a variety of plant collections, as well as a lush peony garden, which blooms in early summer.

ENTERTAINMENT AND EVENTS
Nightlife
Like many college towns, Ann Arbor offers up some eclectic nightlife. The **Blind Pig** (208 S. 1st St., 734/996-8555, www.blindpigmusic.com, Wed.-Mon., show times and ticket prices vary) was one of the first clubs outside of Seattle to give Nirvana a boost; besides rock 'n' roll, the hip space features reggae and blues artists. The city's gay community convenes Friday night at the New York-style **Necto** (516 E. Liberty, 734/994-5436, www.necto.com, 9pm-2am Mon. and Thurs.-Sat., cover charges vary), a dance club that features a different theme each night, including industrial, top 40, and gay.

One of the best known of Ann Arbor's clubs is **The Ark** (316 S. Main St., 734/761-1451, www.a2ark.org, show times and ticket prices vary), a 400-seat venue that has been hosting local, national, and international acoustic performers since 1965. The club moved to larger digs on South Main in the former Kline's Department Store several years ago, but the philosophy is the same: Book the best of folk and roots musicians. Period.

The Arts
The University of Michigan is a hotbed of live

music and other performing arts. If you're interested in such cultural pursuits, contact the **University Musical Society** (UMS, 734/764-2538, www.ums.org, show times and ticket prices vary), which oversees a wide assortment of choral and chamber concerts, dance and theatrical performances, jazz and piano series, even family-friendly shows. Performance venues are situated throughout the campus, including the **Lydia Mendelssohn Theatre** (911 N. University Ave.), the **Hill Auditorium** (825 N. University Ave.), and the **Power Center for the Performing Arts** (121 Fletcher St.), among others.

Ann Arbor Summer Festival
For three weeks each summer (usually mid-June-early July), the **Ann Arbor Summer Festival** (734/994-5999, www.annarborsummerfestival.com) presents a dizzying array of concerts, dance performances, films, exhibitions, parties, and other activities throughout Ann Arbor. The festival, a beloved community event for over 25 years, features an eclectic mix of performers, which, in recent years, has

Ann Arbor Street Art Fair

included Mandy Patinkin, Garrison Keillor, Willie Nelson, and the Funk Brothers.

Another beloved summertime event is the **Ann Arbor Street Art Fair** (734/994-5260, www.artfair.org), which usually takes place during a four-day weekend in mid-July. Founded in 1960, this is the oldest of the four art fairs that now take place in Ann Arbor. For many residents and out-of-towners, it's also the best, luring an impressive collective of painters, photographers, sculptors, woodworkers, jewelry makers, and other artists from around the world to the streets of downtown Ann Arbor.

SHOPPING

The area along State Street remains the main campus commercial strip, with a funky mix of coffeehouses, bookstores, and urbane boutiques. A standout is the historic 1915 **Nickels Arcade**, a small, European-style arcade filled with ever-changing boutiques and galleries between State and Maynard. One longtime favorite is **Bivouac** (336 S. State St., 734/761-6207, www.bivouacannarbor.com, hours vary), the resource for Ann Arbor-area campers, hikers, climbers, and skiers.

More shopping is concentrated on and around **Main Street** (www.mainstreetannarbor.org) in the city's vintage downtown. Once a mainstay of longtime German businesses, it has since become a stylish place for browsing, people-watching, and noshing. The **Selo/Shevel Gallery** (301 S. Main St., 734/761-4620, www.seloshevelgallery.com, 11am-7pm Mon.-Thurs. and Sat., 11am-10pm Fri., noon-6pm Sun.) has one of the state's best collections of handmade contemporary jewelry as well as a nice selection of art glass. Try **Falling Water Books & Collectables** (213 S. Main St., 734/747-9810, www.fallingwatermi.com, 10am-9pm Mon.-Thurs., 10am-10pm Fri.-Sat., 11am-7pm Sun.) for arty gifts, journals, jewelry, candles, and other New Age goodies.

Kerrytown District

Once forlorn and forgotten, this old commercial strip north of downtown is enjoying its second go-round as a retail district, boasting

the impressive **Peoples Food Co-op** (216 N. 4th Ave., 734/994-9174, www.peoplesfood.coop, 8am-10pm Mon.-Sat., 9am-10pm Sun.), Ann Arbor's only community-owned grocery store. Two other popular shopping options are the colorful (if pricey) open-air **Ann Arbor Farmers Market** (315 Detroit St., 734/994-3276, www.a2gov.org/market, 7am-3pm Wed. and Sat.), where early risers will find the finest flowers and produce, and the **Ann Arbor Artisan Market** (317 S. Division St., 734/913-9622, www.artisanmarket.org, 11am-4pm Sun.), a find for arts-and-crafts lovers.

Top restaurants and interesting indoor shops also lure visitors into the **Kerrytown Market & Shops** (415 N. 5th Ave., 734/662-5008, www.kerrytown.com, shop hours vary), where you can browse through boutiques such as **Mudpuddles**, a kids' store featuring puppets, wildlife mobiles, award-winning games, and other delights; the gourmet-inspired **Everyday Cook;** the 5,000-square-foot **Hollander's,** the premier place for decorative paper and bookbinding supplies; and **Mathilde's Imports**, offering a unique selection of women's apparel from Latin America, Europe, and Southeast Asia. For more information about this one-of-a-kind shopping district, contact the **Kerrytown District Association** (www.kerrytown.org).

COLLEGE SPORTS

If you're a sports fan visiting Ann Arbor during the fall football season, you might consider catching a U of M Wolverines game, which can be a rousing all-day affair. For information about tickets and schedules—or for details about any university sporting event, from baseball to ice hockey—contact the **University of Michigan Athletics Ticket Office** (1000 S. State St., 734/764-0247, www.mgoblue.com, 8:30am-5pm Mon.-Fri., ticket prices vary).

ACCOMMODATIONS
Under $150

Lodgings in Ann Arbor aren't as varied as the entertainment or dining options. Most are chain hotels that can't be missed on your way into town. The 223-room **Holiday Inn** (3600

Plymouth Rd., 734/769-9800, www.ichotels-group.com, $106-180 d), for instance, has an indoor pool, a fitness center, a beauty salon, laundry facilities, and high-speed Internet access, plus convenient in-room coffeemakers and irons. A more affordable option is the pet-friendly **Comfort Inn & Suites** (2376 Carpenter Rd., 734/477-9977, www.comfortinn.com, $80-157 d), which offers 50 comfortable rooms, an indoor pool and exercise room, free wireless Internet access, and other basic amenities.

On the eastern edge of town, the **Clarion Hotel and Conference Center** (2900 Jackson Rd., 734/665-4444, www.clarionhotel.com, $80-130 d), a full-service, pet-friendly hotel, provides an indoor/outdoor pool, a sauna, a fitness center, a restaurant and lounge, cable television, complimentary Internet access, and abundant free parking. To the south lies the elegant **[Sheraton Ann Arbor** (3200 Boardwalk, 734/996-0600, www.sheratonannarbor.com, $114-185 d), with its fitness center, sauna, heated pool, gift shop, excellent steakhouse, and 197 tasteful guest rooms.

Budget-conscious travelers will appreciate the **Lamp Post Inn** (2424 E. Stadium Blvd., 734/971-8000 or 877/971-8001, www.lamppostinn.com, $49-79 d), which offers a free continental breakfast, comfortable rooms with complimentary wireless Internet access, and convenient shopping at the adjacent Lamp Post Plaza. For history buffs, the restored **[Vitosha Guest Haus** (1917 Washtenaw Ave., 734/741-4969, $75-149 d) promises more than just 11 old-fashioned rooms, Internet access, a deluxe breakfast, afternoon tea, English-style gardens, and a pet-friendly policy; the stone chalet was built by Dr. Dean Meyer in 1917 and occupied by Unitarians before becoming a sophisticated cultural retreat, a favorite among artists and scholars.

$150-250

For a unique option, consider the intimate **[Bell Tower Hotel** (300 S. Thayer, 734/769-3010, www.belltowerhotel.com, $169-210 d), which offers 66 rooms and suites, right in the

middle of campus. It's a surprisingly elegant place, with accommodations decorated in a crisp, traditional English style, as well as the on-site Mercy's at the Bell Tower, one of the city's finest French restaurants.

If you prefer the coziness of a bed-and-breakfast, the **Ann Arbor Bed & Breakfast** (921 E. Huron St., 734/994-9100, www.annarborbedandbreakfast.com, $159-229 d) might suit your needs. Just steps from some of the university's finest performance venues, the inn features hearty breakfasts, wireless Internet access, and free covered parking. Two of the guest studios even come with kitchenettes.

FOOD

Ann Arbor, along with surrounding Washtenaw County, is home to more than 275 restaurants, a number seldom found in comparably sized cities.

Downtown

Reliable choices in downtown Ann Arbor include **Afternoon Delight** (251 E. Liberty, 734/665-7513, www.afternoondelightcafe.com, 8am-3pm Mon.-Sat., 8:30am-3pm Sun., $4-9), an ideal spot for homemade soups, deli sandwiches, and scrumptious desserts, and **Amadeus Restaurant** (122 E. Washington, 734/665-8767, www.amadeusrestaurant.com, 11:30am-2:30pm and 5pm-10pm Tues.-Thurs., 11:30am-2:30pm and 5pm-11pm Fri., 11:30am-11pm Sat., 11am-3pm Sun., $15-24), a cozy European-inspired café and patisserie that features hearty Polish, central European, and vegetarian entrées.

Another nearby favorite is **[Gratzi** (326 S. Main St., 734/663-6387, www.gratzirestaurant.com, 11:30am-10pm Mon.-Thurs., 11:30am-11pm Fri.-Sat., 4pm-9pm Sun., $9-30), serving up Northern Italian fare in a vintage 1920s theater. For the best view of the large, Bacchanalian murals, sit in the balcony. If you'd prefer lighter fare, such as terrific coffee, pastries, and gourmet sandwiches, head for **Café Felix** (204 S. Main St., 734/662-8650, www.cafefelix.com, 11am-midnight Mon.-Thurs., 11am-1am Fri., 9am-1am Sat.,

THE HEARTLAND

© DANIEL MARTONE

THE HEARTLAND

the Heidelberg Restaurant

9am-10pm Sun., $7-18), a pleasant European-style bistro and Ann Arbor's first full-menu tapas bar.

North of Downtown

To the north, you'll find the three-story **Heidelberg Restaurant** (215 N. Main St., 734/663-7758, www.heidelbergannarbor.com, 11am-10pm Mon.-Thurs., 11am-midnight Fri.-Sat., 3pm-2am Sun., $9-18), an integral part of Ann Arbor's fine dining tradition since the early 1960s. The basement level, the Rathskeller, serves as a traditional German bar; the main dining room presents German specialties like sauerbrauten and Wiener schnitzel; and the top floor, The Club Above, offers live entertainment seven nights a week.

Kerrytown District

Head a few blocks into the Kerrytown District, where you shouldn't miss **Zingerman's Delicatessen** (422 Detroit St., 734/663-3354, www.zingermansdeli.com, 7am-10pm daily,

$5-19), a story in itself. Gastronomes and food critics alike consider this New York-style deli the best deli in the Midwest—maybe the nation. Most head for the deli counter, offering more than 100 sandwiches, side salads, and fragrant imported cheeses. The grocery side of the store has homemade breads and surrounding shelves stocked with the best of everything, from jams to olive oils. The grocery counter is busiest on weekday mornings, after work, and all day on weekends; the sandwich area is mobbed for lunch and dinner. Consider calling ahead, to have your order waiting, and plan on eating at the relaxed Zingerman's Next Door, where you can linger as long as you want over a meal.

Around the University of Michigan

If you're looking for a decent breakfast spot near campus, consider **Angelo's** (1100 E. Catherine, 734/761-8996, www.angelosa2.com, 6am-3pm Mon.-Sat., 7am-2pm Sun., $5-10), the hands-down favorite for their famous deep-fried French toast, made with homemade raisin bread and loaded with fresh berries. For a more sophisticated dining experience, reserve a table at the **Gandy Dancer** (401 Depot St., 734/769-0592, www.muer.com, 11am-10pm Mon.-Thurs., 11am-11pm Fri., 4:30pm-11pm Sat., 10am-9pm Sun., $22-50), part of the Muer seafood restaurant chain. Housed inside the restored 1886 Michigan Central Depot, this elegant restaurant showcases creative seafood dishes like wasabi pea-encrusted tuna and pan-seared jumbo sea scallops with smoked bacon and asparagus. The delectable Sunday brunch features live jazz.

INFORMATION AND SERVICES

For more information about Ann Arbor, contact the **Ann Arbor Area Convention & Visitors Bureau** (120 W. Huron St., 734/995-7281, www.annarbor.org, 8:30am-5pm Mon.-Fri.) or the **Ann Arbor Area Chamber of Commerce** (115 W. Huron St., 3rd Fl.,

734/665-4433, www.annarborchamber.org, 9am-5pm Mon.-Fri.). For information about Washtenaw County, visit www.ewashtenaw. org. For local news and entertainment, consult *Ann Arbor.com* (www.annarbor.com) or **WCBN** (88.3 FM, www.wcbn.org), the University of Michigan's student-run radio station.

Sizable Ann Arbor offers all the services required by travelers, from grocery stores to banks to pharmacies. For mailing needs, stop by one of Ann Arbor's many **post offices** (200 E. Liberty St., 734/662-2009, www.usps. com). As a college town, Ann Arbor is also a terrific place to snag free wireless Internet access, so find a coffee shop, such as **Café Verde** (734/994-9174, www.peoplesfood.coop, daily), and start surfing.

In case of an emergency that requires police, fire, or ambulance services, dial **911** from any cell or public phone. For medical assistance, consult the **University of Michigan Health System** (1500 E. Medical Center Dr., 734/936-4000, www.med.umich.edu).

GETTING THERE AND AROUND

Reaching Ann Arbor is a snap. Both **Amtrak** (325 Depot St., 800/872-7245, www.amtrak.com) and **Greyhound** (116 W. Huron St., 734/662-5511 or 800/231-2222, www.greyhound.com) serve the city. In addition, you can fly into the **Detroit Metropolitan-Wayne County Airport** (DTW, 1 Detroit Metropolitan Airport Tram, Detroit, 734/247-7678, www.metroairport.com), rent a vehicle from one of eight national car rental agencies, and head west on I-94 to Ann Arbor, a 26-mile trip that, without traffic, will take about a half hour. Of course, you can also hitch a ride from **Metro Airport Taxi** (800/745-5191, www.metroairporttaxi.org), which costs about $42-49 for a trip between the Detroit airport and Ann Arbor.

Not surprisingly, motorists can reach Ann Arbor from a variety of directions. From Flint, for instance, you can take I-69 West to I-75 South, continue onto US-23 South, merge onto M-14 West, and follow the US-23 South Business Route into Ann Arbor, a 55-mile trip that, without traffic, will take about 53 minutes. From Chicago, meanwhile, you can take I-90 East and I-94 East to reach Ann Arbor, passing through towns like Kalamazoo, Battle Creek, Marshall, and Jackson; without traffic, this 240-mile trip will require just over 3.5 hours. Just be advised that, en route from the Windy City, parts of I-90 East and I-94 East serve as the Indiana Toll Road.

Once you arrive in Ann Arbor, though, you'll discover that it's a walking town. Residents who don't have cars (as well as the majority of students at the University of Michigan) use foot power or zip around town on bikes or in-line skates. There's also a reliable public bus system, the **Ann Arbor Transportation Authority** (734/996-0400 or 734/973-6500, www.theride.org, one-way $1.50 adults, $0.75 students 6-18, children under 6 and seniors free), which delivers passengers around the main campus as well as farther afield. In addition, you can also depend on **Ann Arbor Taxi** (734/883-6921, www.annarbortaxi.com), which offers service to and from the Detroit airport as well as transportation around the Ann Arbor area and other parts of southeastern Michigan.

Naturally, you can also drive around the Ann Arbor area. Whether you've brought your own car or a rental, watch for the easy-access parking garages spread throughout the city. There's also plenty of street parking available, but be aware that the city has very thorough parking enforcement officers. In other words, bring plenty of change for the parking meters and make note of any instructive signs.

YPSILANTI

Not far from Ann Arbor, you'll encounter the town of Ypsilanti. Besides being the home of **Eastern Michigan University** (EMU, 734/487-1849, www.emich.edu), Ypsilanti features two unique museums. The **Michigan Firehouse Museum** (110 W. Cross St., 734/547-0663, www.michiganfirehousemuseum.org, 10am-4pm Tues.-Sat., noon-4pm Sun., $5 adults, $3

THE HEARTLAND

THE HEARTLAND

© LYNDA HUMMEL

cruise nights in Ypsilanti

children 2-16, children under 2 free) offers a look at Michigan's firefighting history, while also promoting fire safety and prevention. The **Ypsilanti Historical Museum** (220 N. Huron St., 734/484-0080 or 734/482-4990, www. ypsilantihistoricalsociety.org, 2pm-5pm Tues.-Sun., free) provides a glimpse of Ypsilanti's history since its founding in 1860.

Also in Ypsilanti, you'll find the **Riverside Arts Center** (76 N. Huron St., 734/480-2787, www.riversidearts.org), which presents exhibits and performances in the theater space. For a bite to eat, visit **Aubree's Pizzeria & Tavern** (39 E. Cross St., 734/483-1870, www.aubrees. com, 11am-2am Mon.-Sat., noon-2am Sun., $7-17), which offers a variety of comfort foods and pizza selections.

For more information about the Ypsilanti area, consult the **Ypsilanti Area Convention & Visitors Bureau** (106 W. Michigan Ave., 734/483-4444, www.visitypsinow.com). To reach the town itself, simply take Washtenaw Avenue from Ann Arbor; without traffic, the eight-mile trip should take about 18 minutes.

CHELSEA

Considered by many to be little more than a trendy suburb of neighboring Ann Arbor, Chelsea has begun to make a name for itself, thanks to a big-name Hollywood star who still resides in this picturesque little town, and a big swath of public land just west of town.

◖ Purple Rose Theatre Company

When he's not off making movies, actor Jeff Daniels eschews the Tinseltown glitz for his hometown of Chelsea. Despite a crammed film schedule, Daniels keeps busy running the **Purple Rose Theatre Company** (137 Park St., 734/433-7673, www.purplerosetheatre.org, box office 10am-6pm Mon.-Fri., show days noon-10pm Sat., noon-4pm Sun., $20-40 pp), which he founded in 1991, naming it after the Woody Allen film *The Purple Rose of Cairo*, in which he'd starred six years prior. This critically acclaimed regional playhouse features classic plays such as *A Streetcar Named Desire* as well as modern works, even plays written by Daniels himself.

JEFF DANIELS: MICHIGAN'S TOP PROMOTER

Certainly one of the more recognizable faces in Michigan, actor Jeff Daniels has been gracing movie screens for more than three decades. In 2008, he also appeared in a television commercial for the Michigan Economic Development Corporation, part of a national campaign to promote Michigan's tourism and business opportunities.

Born in Athens, Georgia, in 1955, Jeffrey Warren Daniels grew up in Chelsea, Michigan, where his family has owned a lumber company since the 1920s. After marrying his high school sweetheart in 1979, he began to pursue an acting career. Some of his early films included *Terms of Endearment* (1983), *The Purple Rose of Cairo* (1985), and *Arachnophobia* (1990).

In 1991, he founded the Purple Rose Theatre Company in his hometown of Chelsea. Although he, his wife, and his three grown children still consider Michigan home, Daniels has continued to work in Hollywood, turning in memorable performances in films like *Gettysburg* (1993), *Speed* (1994), *Pleasantville* (1998), *Blood Work* (2002), *Imaginary Heroes* (2004), *The Lookout* (2007), *Howl* (2009), and *Looper* (2012), not to mention the TV series *The Newsroom* (2012-present).

Even with such success, Daniels has never forgotten his Midwestern roots. In 2001, he wrote, directed, and starred in *Escanaba in da Moonlight*, a quirky comedy about deer-hunting season in the Upper Peninsula. Despite an incredibly busy film schedule, he's also lent his voice to radio spots that promote Michigan tourism and used his well-known persona to lure businesses here. While some residents find it hard to be hopeful in times of downsizing auto factories and an uncertain economy, many have appreciated his sincerity and commitment. It's admirable, after all, that a movie star as famous as Jeff Daniels would eschew the Hollywood scene and use his celebrity status to support the people of his home state.

THE HEARTLAND

After catching a show at this landmark theater, head to the town's other big-name attraction: **The Common Grill** (112 S. Main St., 734/475-0470, www.commongrill.com, 11am-10pm Tues.-Thurs., 11am-11pm Fri.-Sat., 11am-9pm Sun., $10-30), a superb restaurant founded in 1991 by former employees of Detroit's Chuck Muer restaurant chain. The Grill helped put sleepy Chelsea on the map, and waits easily reach two hours on weekends. Folks come for the signature fish dishes and the chic yet comfortable atmosphere, which includes painted Hopperesque scenes of old Chelsea (including the Jiffy Baking Company's tower) on the exposed brick walls.

Waterloo Recreation Area

Sprawling across two counties and some 20,000 acres, the Waterloo Recreation Area (16345 McClure Rd., 734/475-8307, www.michigan.gov/dnr, hours vary daily, annual $11 Recreation Passport for Michigan residents or $8.40 day-use fee/$30.50 yearly Recreation Passport for nonresidents required) counts as the largest park in the Lower Peninsula. The park's landscape clearly shows evidence of the glaciers that once blanketed this part of the state. Waterloo is located at the intersection of the Kalamazoo and the Missaukee moraine systems, where two glaciers collided thousands of years ago. The ice sheets ripped apart massive mountains of rock from the Canadian shield to the north, carrying fragments with them as the ice moved across this part of the state—a journey one park interpreter has described as "the movement of pancake batter on a hot griddle."

The area is a pleasing patchwork of field, forest, and lake. Pick up a map at park headquarters to help you navigate around this expansive place, which contains 11 fishing lakes, several beaches and picnic areas, and miles of hiking, biking, equestrian, and cross-country skiing trails. Here, you'll also find the year-round

Gerald E. Eddy Discovery Center, which offers engaging exhibits about Michigan's geologic features, and the 1,000-acre **Haehnle Audubon Sanctuary,** a favorite fall hangout of sandhill cranes.

Waterloo maintains four campgrounds in all ($12-24 daily). Equestrian (for campers with horses) and Green Lake are rustic areas, with nice wooded sites. Portage Lake and Sugarloaf are large, modern campgrounds, with sites near (but not on) their namesake lakes.

Information

For more information about Chelsea, consult the **Chelsea Area Chamber of Commerce** (310 N. Main St., Ste. 120, 734/475-1145, www.chelseamichamber.org, 10am-4pm Mon.-Fri.).

Getting There and Around

Chelsea is situated about halfway between Ann Arbor and Jackson, so it's easily accessible via car, motorcycle, or RV. From downtown Ann Arbor, for instance, head north on the I-94 Business Route, take I-94 West to exit 159, and follow M-52 North to Chelsea; without traffic, the 17-mile trip should take about 23 minutes. From Jackson, take I-94 East to M-52 North, which will take you directly to Chelsea; without traffic, this 24-mile trip usually takes about 29 minutes. Once here, you can park the car and take a stroll (or ride a bike) through the downtown area.

Jackson and Vicinity

If you're looking for Michigan's liberal stronghold, don't look in Jackson. The Republican Party was founded in this small city of 33,400 back in 1854. More than a thousand Free Soilers, Whigs, and Democrats gathered here, where they adopted the Republican name, issued a platform, and nominated candidates for state office. A tablet still marks the site at the corner of Franklin and 2nd Streets. The Jackson area has also been home to several astronauts. Moreover, it has often claimed fame as "Nuge Country," a nod to Ted Nugent, rocker and bow hunter extraordinaire, who lives nearby. As if that isn't enough, Jackson holds the Midwest's largest and oldest Civil War muster each August, attracting more than 1,200 costumed reenactors from across the country who gather here for battle, balls, and ballistics.

Like many once-booming industrial cities in mid-Michigan, downtown Jackson was hit hard by unemployment and the "malling" of America. Few shops still occupy the city's stately Victorian and art deco storefronts. Even Jacobson's—the posh department store chain founded in Jackson, with stores that once stretched to Florida—closed its downtown store here and eventually filed for bankruptcy in 2002.

But even a flat economy can't affect the wealth of wonderful lakes in surrounding Jackson County. Hundreds of natural lakes dot the countryside, keeping the Jackson area near the top of the list for those in southern Michigan and northern Indiana looking for an easy weekend getaway. Area golf courses, museums, antiques shops, and vineyards only sweeten the deal for many vacationers.

SIGHTS
Ella Sharp Museum of Art and History

Trace the development of the Jackson area at the **Ella Sharp Museum of Art and History** (3225 4th St., 517/787-2320, www.ellasharp.org, 10am-5pm Tues.-Wed. and Fri.-Sat., 10am-7pm Thurs., galleries $5 adults, $3 children 5-12, children under 5 free, house tours $3 adults, $3 children 5-12, children under 5 free). Sharp's mother was a rich expatriate who had invested in western Michigan land in the 1800s and later came to live on it—a rarity, since most investors were absentee landlords. Ella, born in Jackson, grew into a successful reformer who worked to improve rural life through good government, women's associations, and conservation. She also was a pack rat, so plenty of 19th-century artifacts and memorabilia fill this museum complex, which includes Ella Sharp's 1857 farmhouse, an 1840 log cabin, a one-room schoolhouse, and the Midwest's finest wildlife art collection.

The Cascades

Perhaps in response to the awe-inspiring waterfalls of the Upper Peninsula, Jackson has one of the largest man-made waterfalls in North America. Better known as **The Cascades** (1992 Warren Ave., 517/788-4320, 11am-11pm daily May-Sept., $3 pp, children under 6 free), were a creation of "Captain" William Sparks, a well-known area industrialist, philanthropist, and former mayor. This is truly an amazing slice of Americana: 18 separate falls up to 500 feet high, six fountains of various heights and patterns, 1,200 colored lights, and choreographed show tunes. Kids especially love it. The falls and surrounding 465-acre Sparks County Park date back to the early 1930s, when Sparks, a three-time mayor and chamber of commerce president, developed the whole shebang and presented it as a gift to his beloved city. You can make a day of it here, since the falls are augmented by a golf course, a picnic area, fishing ponds, tennis courts, and paddleboat rentals.

Southeast Michigan Pioneer Wine Trail

While the winemaking region of southeastern Michigan is no match for the wineries that line the Southwest Coast and surround Grand Traverse Bay, connoisseurs will still appreciate the selections that constitute the **Southeast Michigan Pioneer Wine Trail** (www.pioneerwinetrail.com). In Jackson, you'll find **Sandhill Crane Vineyards** (4724 Walz Rd., 517/764-0679, www.sandhillcranevineyards.com, 11am-6pm Mon.-Sat., noon-6pm Sun.), an award-winning, family-owned winery with a year-round tasting room. Other area wineries include the **Lone Oak Vineyard Estate** (8400 Ann Arbor Rd., Grass Lake, 517/522-8167,

www.loneoakvineyards.com, noon-7pm daily), established in 1997 and offering complimentary tastings, and the **Pentamere Winery** (131 E. Chicago Blvd., Tecumseh, 517/423-9000, www.pentamerewinery.com, 11am-7pm Tues.-Fri., 10am-7pm Sat., noon-5pm Sun.), where you can even take classes on the techniques of tasting and evaluating wines.

FESTIVALS AND EVENTS

The **Ella Sharp Museum of Art and History** (3225 4th St., 517/787-2320, www.ellasharp.org) holds three interesting annual events: the **Sugar & Shearing Festival,** a late March event that celebrates the arrival of springtime with sheep-shearing and maple sugar demonstrations; the **Art & Wine Festival,** which invites visitors to the museum grounds in early June for the chance to sample area wines and peruse regional artwork; and the **Fall Harvest Festival,** an October event that celebrates autumn with pumpkin painting, a farmers market, and an antique tractor trade.

For something completely different, plan a trip around the annual **Hot Air Jubilee** (Jackson County Airport, 3606 Wildwood Ave., 517/782-1515, www.hotairjubilee.com, $10 adults, children 6-12 free) in mid-July. Watching nearly 70 colorful hot air balloons take to the sky at once is quite a dazzling sight. Besides the balloons, the weekend features an arts-and-crafts show, stunt kite demonstrations, carnival rides, aircraft and antique military displays, and live entertainment. Stick around until sunset for the Balloon Night Glow, a spectacular light show of tethered balloons.

SPORTS AND RECREATION

Michigan International Speedway

The **Michigan International Speedway** (12626 US-12, Brooklyn, 517/592-6666, www.mispeedway.com, racing times and ticket prices vary), which opened in 1968, offers one of the country's premier auto racing facilities. Featuring over 80,000 seats and a large RV campground, the track presents NASCAR races (for the Truck, Sprint Cup, and Nationwide series) mid-June- mid-August. In addition, the speedway often presents official driving schools during the warmer months, so if you have a lead foot, perhaps you should try some legal speeding instead.

Golf

The Jackson area is nuts for golf and hides a number of high-quality public courses. Two good choices are the **Arbor Hills Golf Club** (1426 Arbor Hills Rd., 517/750-2290, www.arborhillsgolf.com, daily Apr.-Oct., $22-28 pp w/ cart), formerly a private club for over 80 years, and the **Cascades Golf Course** (1992 Warren Ave., 517/788-4323, www.cascadesgolfcourse.com, daily Apr.-Oct., $27-35 pp w/cart), established in 1929 and voted Jackson's best golf course in 2007.

ACCOMMODATIONS AND FOOD

You'll find a range of reasonably priced chain hotels clustered near the I-94 interchange in Jackson. Three include the **Hampton Inn** (2225 Shirley Dr., 517/789-5151, www.hamptoninn.com, $119-139 d), the **Fairfield Inn** (2395 Shirley Dr., 517/784-7877, www.marriott.com, $94-149 d), and the **Country Hearth Inn** (1111 Boardman Rd., 517/783-6404, www.countryhearth.com, $63-83 d).

This is meat-and-potatoes country, and you're going to have a tough time beating it. If you're happy to join it, try **Steve's Ranch** (311 Louis Glick Hwy., 517/787-4367, www.stevesranch.com, 6am-10pm Mon.-Sat., 6am-8pm Sun., $10-30), a longtime favorite for omelets, burgers, and, of course, steaks.

INFORMATION AND SERVICES

For more information about Jackson, contact the **Jackson County Convention & Visitors Bureau** (141 S. Jackson St., 517/764-4440, www.visitjacksonmi.com, 8am-5pm Mon.-Fri.) or the **Greater Jackson Chamber of Commerce** (141 S. Jackson St., 517/782-8221, www.gjcc.org, 8am-5pm Mon.-Fri.). For local news and events, consult the *Jackson Citizen Patriot* (www.mlive.com/citpat).

For groceries and prescriptions, stop by **Meijer** (3333 E. Michigan Ave., 517/787-8722, www.meijer.com), part of an enormous regional chain. For mailing needs, visit one of Jackson's many **post offices** (113 W. Michigan Ave., 517/768-0611, www.usps.com), and for banking assistance, consult **Flagstar** (www.flagstar.com), which has several branches in town.

In case of an emergency, dial **911** from any cell or public phone. For medical services, consult **Allegiance Health** (205 N. East Ave., 517/788-4800, www.allegiancehealth.org).

GETTING THERE AND AROUND

Both **Amtrak** (501 E. Michigan Ave., 800/872-7245, www.amtrak.com) and **Greyhound** (127 W. Cortland, 517/789-6148 or 800/231-2222, www.greyhound.com) serve Jackson. In addition, the town is situated halfway between the **Detroit Metropolitan-Wayne County Airport** (DTW, 1 Detroit Metropolitan Airport Tram, Detroit, 734/247-7678, www.metroairport.com) and the **Kalamazoo/Battle Creek International Airport** (AZO, 5235 Portage Rd., Kalamazoo, 269/388-3668, www.azoairport.com), from which you can easily rent a vehicle and head to Jackson via I-94. From the Detroit airport, for instance, you can simply take I-94 West to exit 139, turn left onto M-106 South, and head 2 miles south to downtown Jackson; without traffic, this 61-mile trip will take you about an hour. From the Kalamazoo airport, meanwhile, you can just take I-94 East to exit 138, turn right onto M-50 East/US-127 South Business Route, and head a couple of miles into downtown Jackson; without traffic, this 64-mile trip will take you about an hour.

Of course, if you've driven to Michigan, there are a number of other ways to reach Jackson. From Lansing, for example, you can follow I-496 East for 5 miles, and then head to Jackson via M-50 East/US-127 South Business Route; without traffic, the 39-mile trip will take about 40 minutes. Once you reach Jackson, you can drive, bike, or even walk around town. It's also possible to rely on the **Jackson Area Transportation Authority** (JATA, 517/787-8363, www.jacksontransit.com, one-way $1.50 adults, $1 students, $0.75 seniors and children), which offers bus service around the Jackson area.

THE IRISH HILLS AND LENAWEE COUNTY

Southeast of Jackson via US-127 South and US-12 East, the lovely Irish Hills have long been a popular family getaway, dotted with summer cottages owned by residents of Michigan, Indiana, and Ohio. The area was formed during the last ice age, when huge ice chunks swept across the land, leaving behind a varied landscape of round kettle-hole lakes, steep valleys, and picturesque sweeping meadows. It got its name from Irish settlers who thought the region resembled their homeland.

You can enjoy the area's natural state at **W.J. Hayes State Park** (1220 Wamplers Lake Rd., Onsted, 517/467-7401, www.michigan.gov/dnr, hours vary daily, annual $11 Recreation Passport for Michigan residents or $8.40 day-use fee/$30.50 yearly Recreation Passport for nonresidents required). The 654-acre park, which lies 23 miles southeast of Jackson and isn't far from the Michigan International Speedway, features two popular fishing lakes tucked amid gentle rolling hills. Facilities include a sandy swimming beach, a boat launch, a picnic area, and 185 modern campsites.

Nearby, the **Cambridge Junction Historic State Park** (13220 M-50, Brooklyn, 517/467-4414, hours vary, free) features the 1832 **Walker Tavern,** which tells the story of the spine-crunching Chicago Road, the chief route of settlement during the 1830s pioneer boom. Now a fine small state historical museum, it illustrates how travelers once piled into the tavern's few sleeping rooms, shared beds, and passed much of their time in the 1st-floor bar and dining room. Daniel Webster and James Fenimore Cooper stayed here on expeditions west.

Information

For more information about the Irish Hills, contact the **Lenawee County Conference & Visitors Bureau** (209 N. Main St., Adrian, 517/263-7747, www.visitlenawee.com).

Marshall

When Lansing was chosen as the seat of the state government in 1847, no city was more surprised and more disappointed than Marshall, located 31 miles west of Jackson. The State Senate originally passed a bill designating Marshall the capital, a measure defeated by just one vote in the House. Marshall was so sure of its upcoming role as the capital city that it set aside a site known as Capitol Hill. It even built a governor's mansion, which still exists today.

Being spurned by the legislature, though, gave Marshall a reprieve from rampant development, and today it ranks as one of the country's best-preserved 19th-century towns, with just under 7,100 residents. Lined by large shade trees and an outstanding collection of 1840s and 1850s Greek and Gothic Revival-style homes, house-proud Marshall has become a poster child for historic preservation, an example of what can be done when businesses and homeowners work together. The town has been featured in dozens of travel articles and architectural magazines. "Marshall's small-town pride is a genteel descendant of the boosterism that Sinclair Lewis savaged in *Main Street* and *Babbitt,*" once declared the *New York Times.*

Before Marshall was old enough to turn heads for its architecture, it was carving out a niche as a center of the patent medicine boom in the early 1900s, producer of such classic tonics as Lydia Pinkham's Pink Pills for Pale People. It wasn't until the 1920s that a savvy mayor, Harold Brooks, first recognized the city's fine architecture and led a crusade to maintain it. The first home tour was held in 1964 and remains a large and popular annual event half a century later. Marshall's designated National Historic Landmark District includes over 850 homes and businesses, the country's largest district in the "small urban" category. One National Park Service manager called Marshall "a textbook of 19th-century small-town architecture."

There's a rich and controversial history hiding behind those pretty 19th-century facades, too. Marshall drew nationwide attention in 1846 when Adam Crosswhite, a slave who had escaped from Kentucky and lived in Marshall for two years, was seized by slave hunters. The whole town rose up in his support. Local abolitionists helped Crosswhite and his family escape to Canada, arrested the slave hunters, and tried them in Federal District Court. Although the Marshall abolitionists lost in court, the Crosswhite case was instrumental in the creation of the 1850 Fugitive Slave Act, which in turn contributed to the tensions that later caused the Civil War.

SIGHTS
◖ Historic Homes

The best way to see the area's historic homes is on the annual home tour held the weekend after Labor Day. At other times, you can still enjoy the city's architecture with the help of an excellent (and free) walking-tour brochure available at the chamber of commerce and a number of local shops and inns.

One of the first stops should be the lavishly quirky **Honolulu House** (107 N. Kalamazoo Ave., 269/781-8544, www.marshallhistoricalsociety.org, 11am-5pm daily May-Sept., noon-5pm Thurs.-Sun. Oct., $5 pp), home to the Marshall Historical Society and described by the *New York Times* as "the architectural equivalent of a four-rum cocktail served in a coconut." Featuring a pagoda-shaped tower and decorative pineapple trim, the Polynesian-style home was built in 1860 by Michigan Supreme Court judge Abner Pratt, who served as U.S. consul to the Sandwich Islands (now Hawaii) 1857-1859. His wife's poor health forced the couple to return to Marshall, where they brought back their love of the tropics. Pratt's

wife died shortly upon their return, and Pratt himself succumbed to pneumonia soon afterward—perhaps because of his stubborn habit of wearing tropical-weight clothing during the long and cold Midwestern winters.

Inside, the house features 1880s replicas of Pratt's original tropical murals, a riot of purples, pinks, and dozens of other rich colors, and several exquisite fireplaces. Many of the other furnishings did not belong to the Pratts, but represent Marshall history, such as the Marshall Folding Bathtub in the basement. Disguised as a cabinet, it's a rare reminder of the city's patent medicine boom.

Other fine examples of early Marshall architecture can be found two blocks north of the Honolulu House on Kalamazoo Street. They include the home of Mayor Harold Brooks, who spurred the city's revival; the 1857 Italianate Adams-Schuyler-Umphrey House, built on land once owned by James Fenimore Cooper; the 1907 Sears-Osborne House, ordered from the Sears catalog at the turn of the 20th century for just $1,995; the 1886 Queen Anne-style Cronin-Lapietra House, one of the city's most ornate, designed by the Detroit firm best known for the city's Michigan Central Railroad Terminal; and the 1843 Greek Revival Camp-Vernor-Riser House, once home to the founder of Vernor's Ginger Ale.

American Museum of Magic

Renowned magician David Copperfield has called the **American Museum of Magic** (107 E. Michigan Ave., 269/781-7570, www.americanmuseumofmagic.org, by appointment 2nd weekend of each month, $5 adults, $3.50 seniors and children, children under 5 free) one of his "favorite places on earth" and, if you believe the local rumor mill, wants to purchase the museum and move it to Las Vegas. For now, anyway, this fascinating attraction remains in Marshall, housed in a historic 1868 building.

The late Robert Lund, a retired automotive writer, and his wife, Elaine, opened the American Museum of Magic in 1978, after spending years collecting "notional whimsies, cabalistic surprises, phantasmagorical bewilderments, and unparalleled splendors." Roughly translated, that means anything and everything remotely related to the practice of magic. Spanning six continents and over four centuries, this extensive collection of more than 87,000 artifacts and memorabilia includes showbills, programs, books, magazines, photographs, and antique props (even the milk can used by Harry Houdini for a popular escape stunt).

FESTIVALS AND EVENTS

Marshall's must-see event is, of course, the **Annual Historic Home Tour** (269/781-8544, www.marshallhistoricalsociety.org, $15-20 pp), which usually occurs the weekend after Labor Day and is a wonderful way to view hundreds of historic buildings. While strolling along the shady streets of Marshall, visitors can listen to choirs, quartets, and brass bands, the nostalgic sounds of the 19th century.

If you happen to be in town in mid-October, you may be able to check out one of the most unique festivals, **Marshall Scarecrow Days** (800/877-5163). As the name suggests, this weeklong event focuses on scarecrows, scarecrows, and more scarecrows. You'll see a variety of scarecrows in gardens and yards throughout Marshall. There's even a parade that features costumed children and "live" scarecrows.

Southwest of Marshall, Colon's **Magic Get Together** is worth a look, even if you're not a magician. Begun in 1934 as a sales incentive, this annual August gathering of magicians has lured some of the best names in the business, from Harry Blackstone to Lance Burton. For more information, contact **Abbott's Magic Company** (124 St. Joseph St., Colon, 269/432-3235, www.magicgettogether.com, 9am-5pm Mon.-Fri., 9am-4pm Sat.), with its enormous inventory of magic books and supplies.

ANTIQUE SHOPPING

Modern Marshall, with a downtown full of lacy Victorian homes and storefronts, has become an immensely popular weekend getaway for Detroit- and Chicago-area residents. They come to ogle the architecture, shop at a number of well-stocked (if somewhat expensive) antiques stores and malls, and stay in one of the town's historic bed-and-breakfast inns.

You'll find most of the best shops along several blocks of Michigan Avenue and its cross streets. For antiques, try the **Marshall Antique Center** (119 W. Michigan Ave., 269/789-0077, 11am-5pm Tues.-Sat., noon-4pm Sun.), which houses quality dealers in a historic home, or **Keystone Architectural and General Antiques** (110 E. Michigan Ave., 269/789-1355, www.keystoneantiques.com, 1pm-5pm Wed.-Fri. and Sun., 10am-5pm Sat.), with an outstanding collection of vintage furniture, leaded glass, old light fixtures, hand-knotted Persian rugs, and other antique furnishings.

ACCOMMODATIONS AND FOOD

Established in 1835, ◖ **The National House Inn** (102 Parkview, 269/781-7374, www.nationalhouseinn.com, $110-170 d) is the oldest operating inn in the state. This former stagecoach stop along the Chicago Road once served as a station on the Underground Railroad. Guest rooms range from the elegant Victorian-style Ketchum Suite to smaller, pleasant country-style rooms with folk art portraits on the walls. A tip: The old road in front of the inn is now a busy intersection. Ask for a room overlooking the garden if you desire peace and quiet.

Your best budget bet is the **Arbor Inn** (15435 W. Michigan Ave., 269/781-7772, www.arborinnmarshall.com, $45-69 d), a comfortable hotel with an outdoor pool, situated along a strip of fast-food restaurants beyond the historic downtown.

For cheap eats, head to **Louie's Bakery** (144 W. Michigan Ave., 269/781-3542, 5:30am-5pm Mon.-Fri., 5:30am-3:30pm Sat.), the kind of old-fashioned bakery you might remember from childhood, with gooey cakes, pies, and sweet rolls galore.

Wayne and Marjorie Cornwell introduced their first turkey sandwich at a county fair over 40 years ago. Today, their campy, country-style restaurant and turkey farm just north of Marshall is known as ◖ **Cornwell's**

Turkeyville U.S.A. (18935 15½ Mile Rd., 269/781-4293, www.turkeyville.com, 11am-8pm daily, $4-9). The menu includes everything from a classic buttered turkey sandwich to a piled-high turkey Reuben to a turkey stir-fry. An adjacent 170-seat dinner theater presents afternoon and evening performances of family favorites.

INFORMATION AND SERVICES

For more information about Marshall, contact the **Marshall Area Chamber of Commerce** (323 W. Michigan Ave., 269/781-5163 or 800/877-5163, www.marshallmi.org, 8:30am-7pm Mon.-Fri., 10am-4pm Sat.-Sun.). If you require more than just information, you'll find everything you need in surrounding towns like Battle Creek and Jackson, including groceries, pharmacies, gas stations, laundries, and banks. Marshall, too, has its share of businesses, including two **post offices;** consult www.usps.com for locations and hours. In case of an emergency, dial **911** from any cell or public phone. For medical services, visit **Oaklawn Hospital** (200 N. Madison Ave., 269/781-4271, www.oaklawnhospital.org).

GETTING THERE AND AROUND

Marshall is surrounded by several larger towns, such as Battle Creek, Kalamazoo,

East Lansing, Ann Arbor, and Jackson—all of which have bus and train stations, serviced by **Greyhound** (800/231-2222, www.greyhound.com) and **Amtrak** (800/872-7245, www.amtrak.com), respectively. In addition, it's not far from the **Kalamazoo/Battle Creek International Airport** (AZO, 5235 Portage Rd., Kalamazoo, 269/388-3668, www.azoairport.com) and the **Capital Region International Airport** (LAN, 4100 Capital City Blvd., Lansing, 517/321-6121, www.fly-lansing.com), from which you can easily rent a vehicle and head to Marshall via I-94 East and I-69 South, respectively. From the Kalamazoo airport, for instance, you can simply take I-94 East and Old US-27 North to Marshall; the 34-mile trip usually takes about a half hour. From the Lansing airport, meanwhile, you can just take the I-96 West Business Route and I-96 East, continue onto I-69 South, merge onto I-94 East, and follow Old US-27 North to Marshall; without traffic, the 50-mile trip should take you roughly 50 minutes.

Of course, if you've driven to Michigan, there are a number of other ways to reach Marshall, such as taking I-94 West from Ann Arbor, a 65-mile trip that usually requires about an hour, or following I-69 North from Fort Wayne, Indiana, an 89-mile trip that, without traffic, takes about 90 minutes. Once you reach Jackson, you can then drive, bike, or even walk around town.

Battle Creek

To generations of American youngsters, Battle Creek was the home of Tony the Tiger, that g-r-r-r-e-a-t and magical place where they sent their cereal box tops in exchange for free gifts and toys. For decades before that, however, Battle Creek was known as the home of the Church of Seventh-Day Adventists and for the work done at the church's sanitarium, the Western Health Reform Institute, which opened in 1866. John Harvey Kellogg joined the founders in 1876 and spent the next 25 years developing

the sanitarium into an institution recognized around the world for its regimen of hydrotherapy, exercise, and vegetarian diet.

Part of that regimen was a new, healthy, grain-based flaked breakfast that Kellogg cooked up in 1894. An alternative to traditional breakfast foods such as grits, bacon, and eggs, Kellogg's creation went on to revolutionize the breakfast-foods industry and to fuel the economy of this former settlement. From 1901 to 1905, more than 1,500 new homes cropped up

SOJOURNER TRUTH

Described by one biographer as a "riveting preacher and spellbinding singer who dazzled listeners with her wit and originality," Sojourner Truth was born around 1797 as Isabella Baumfree. She spent her childhood and early adulthood as a slave, suffering abuse at the hands of her masters and giving birth to several children. Towering more than six feet, she gained her freedom in New York State in the late 1820s, dropped her given name, and moved west on a "sojourn to preach truth." Her antislavery crusade took her into both small rural churches and the office of President Abraham Lincoln.

She settled in Battle Creek, an abolitionist stronghold, in 1857 and continued to help her people along the Underground Railroad to Canada. While revisionist history has claimed that she never physically assisted runaway slaves, she no doubt inspired many of them with her fiery oratories, which preached economic competence, self-improvement, and social tolerance. A few days before she died in 1883, she said, "I isn't goin' to die, honey, I'se goin' home like a shootin' star." Her funeral was described as the biggest that Battle Creek had ever seen. She is buried in Oak Hill Cemetery by a simple old-fashioned square monument – still a popular pilgrimage spot – just steps away from the ornate marble mausoleum of cereal pioneer C.W. Post.

THE HEARTLAND

to house the workers and others who converged on Battle Creek, hoping to capitalize on its renown as the "Health City." (This bizarre tale was the basis for *The Road to Wellville*, a 1994 Hollywood film starring Anthony Hopkins, which painted a not-too-positive portrait of the Kellogg family and phenomenon.)

Today, Battle Creek is still home to the Kellogg Company as well as Post Cereals (recently transferred from Kraft Foods to Ralcorp). It's also home to the "World's Longest Breakfast Table," a downtown event held as part of the annual Battle Creek Cereal Festival in June.

SIGHTS

Museums and Historic Sites

If you're curious about the Kelloggs, you can visit the sanitarium, now the **Battle Creek Federal Center** (74 N. Washington Ave., 269/961-7015, www.dlis.dla.mil). Recognized on the National Register of Historic Places, the building now houses governmental and military offices, though there are still artifacts and other items on display about the Kellogg era.

If you're looking for an engaging place to take the kids, try the newly renovated **Kingman Museum** (175 Limit St., 269/965-5117, www.

kingmanmuseum.org, 9am-5pm Tues.-Fri., 1pm-5pm Sat., $7 adults, $6 seniors 65 and over, $5 children 3-18). The museum offers a wide array of paleontological and anthropological artifacts, from fossils and skulls to Native American war shields. Visitors can also catch a star show in the new planetarium.

Binder Park Zoo

More modern species can be found at the **Binder Park Zoo** (7400 Division Dr., 269/979-1351, www.binderparkzoo.org, 9am-5pm Mon.-Fri., 9am-6pm Sat., 11am-6pm Sun. late Apr.-mid-Oct., $6 pp Mon.-Fri., $8 pp Sat.-Sun.), a small but choice zoo that houses exotic and domestic animals in natural settings. Highlights include the **Swamp Adventure,** a boardwalk that takes you over bird-filled bogs, marshes, and swamps, and **Wild Africa,** a pseudo-savannah with giraffes, zebras, ostriches, antelope, and other animals of the region.

Parks and Gardens

The Kelloggs preached plenty of fresh air as part of their health regimen. Battle Creek, therefore, excels in its number of parks and recreational opportunities. Among the most unusual is the **Battle Creek Linear Park** (269/966-3431, www.bcparks.org, sunrise-sunset daily), a 17-mile system that links wooded areas, open fields, and parks with a continuous paved pathway. It's a favorite of local cyclists, skaters, and joggers. Walkers and other nature lovers, in particular, head to the **Leila Arboretum** (928 W. Michigan Ave., 269/969-0270, www.leilaarboretumsociety.org, sunrise-sunset daily, free), part of Linear Park. This excellent 72-acre botanical garden is one of the best reasons to visit Battle Creek. The gift of Mrs. Leila Post Montgomery, it contains more than 3,000 species of trees and shrubs (many dating back to the 1920s), laid out in the manner of famous European gardens. Highlights include a rhododendron garden, a breathtaking flowering tree collection, and a children's garden.

FESTIVALS AND EVENTS

Battle Creek hosts several celebrations throughout the year. For over five decades, the **Battle Creek Cereal Festival** has celebrated the city's most famous industry in mid-June with a parade, live entertainment, and the world's longest breakfast table, offering complimentary cereals, fruit juice, and other Kellogg's breakfast foods. Started in 1956 as part of the Kellogg Company's Golden Jubilee, it has become a beloved annual tradition in downtown Battle Creek. Another popular event is the **International Festival of Lights,** during which Linear Park is decorated with lighted holiday displays late November-New Year's Eve. For more information about both events, visit www.bcfestivals.com.

SPORTS AND RECREATION
Golf

If you're visiting Battle Creek during the warmer months and are game for a round of golf, take a drive out to **Gull Lake View Golf Club & Resort** (7417 N. 38th St., Augusta, 269/731-4149 or 800/432-7971, www.gull-lakeview.com, daily Apr.-Oct., $39-57 pp), the oldest and largest golf resort in southwestern Michigan. En route from Battle Creek

to Kalamazoo, this longstanding, family-operated resort offers top-notch lodging and dining, plus five championship golf courses: Gull Lake View East, Gull Lake View West, Stonehedge North, Stonehedge South, and Bedford Valley.

Hiking and Skiing

Naturalists will appreciate the **Kellogg Forest** (7060 N. 42nd St., Augusta, 269/731-4597, 8am-8pm in summer, 8am-sunset in winter, free), begun by cereal king W. K. Kellogg as a demonstration project for reforesting abandoned farms. Michigan State University maintains the 716-acre property as an experimental forest, which includes more than 200 species of trees, 2.5 miles of road, and 35 miles of hiking and cross-country skiing trails. Hikers and skiers also use the forest's 25 miles of ungroomed firebreaks separating experimental stands of trees, and picnickers favor the forest, too.

【 Bird-Watching

Ornithologists and other bird lovers flock to the experimental **W. K. Kellogg Bird Sanctuary** (12685 E. C Ave., Augusta, 269/671-2510, www.kbs.msu.edu, 9am-7pm daily May-Oct., 9am-5pm daily Nov.-Apr., $4 adults, $2 seniors, $1 children 2-12), one of North America's pioneer wildlife conservation centers. W. K. Kellogg started the sanctuary in 1928 as a refuge for Canada geese, which were then threatened by a loss of habitat to agriculture and urbanization. Today, Canada geese thrive at the 180-acre sanctuary, now part of MSU's W. K. Kellogg Biological Station, along with other native waterfowl, including ducks and swans that stay year-round. Also present are several species of raptors and game birds, from red-tailed hawks to pheasants, which you can view from several observation areas on the grounds. Many other species migrate through the region in spring and fall.

Situated along the waterfront of Wintergreen Lake, the grounds can be explored year-round on self-guided trails. A bookstore on-site includes information on how to transform your backyard into a bird sanctuary following the

RETURN OF THE TRUMPETER SWAN

The trumpeter swan, the world's largest waterfowl, can weigh up to 35 pounds when fully grown, with a wingspan of nearly eight feet. Similar in appearance to other white swans, its distinguishing characteristic is its all-black bill. Trumpeter swans typically create large nests in marshy areas, among cattails and other aquatic plants.

Centuries ago, trumpeter swans were abundant throughout the Great Lakes region, even in southern Michigan. In fact, Antoine de la Mothe Cadillac, founder of Detroit, noted their presence along the Detroit River in 1701. As European settlers spread throughout the state, however, the swan population plummeted. During the late 19th century, hunters captured swans for their fine down, while settlers drained crucial marsh habitat. By 1933, only 66 trumpeter swans remained in the continental United States, mainly in remote parts of Alaska and the Rocky Mountains.

During the mid-1980s, Michigan initiated a reintroduction program, intended to establish three self-sustaining populations of at least 200 swans by the year 2000. Despite early failures, biologists were able to incubate eggs collected from zoos and rear the cygnets for two years before releasing them into prime wetland habitat. In 1989, biologists from the Michigan Department of Natural Resources and the W.K. Kellogg Bird Sanctuary traveled to Alaska to collect eggs from wild populations as well.

By 2000, the program was considered a success. At the time, more than 400 trumpeter swans dwelled in Michigan: in the southwestern and northeastern parts of the Lower Peninsula, and in the U.P.'s Seney National Wildlife Refuge.

In recent years, the W.K. Kellogg Bird Sanctuary, which today nurtures over 20 year-round trumpeter swans, has continued reintroduction efforts. Since 2003, the sanctuary has released 28 swans in order to establish breeding populations elsewhere, including 6 that were transported to Sleeping Bear Dunes in 2007. In 2004, Michigan State University conducted a population survey throughout the state; the findings revealed that 655 trumpeter swans were then living in Michigan: roughly 45 percent in the U.P., 26 percent in the Lower Peninsula's northwestern region, and 29 percent in the L.P.'s southern portion.

For more information about conservation efforts, consult the **Michigan Department of Natural Resources** (www.michigan.gov/dnr) or the **W.K. Kellogg Bird Sanctuary** (www.kbs.msu.edu).

THE HEARTLAND

same principles and planting guidelines used in the refuge.

ACCOMMODATIONS AND FOOD

Situated amid rolling meadows, **Greencrest Manor** (6174 Halbert Rd., 269/962-8633, www.greencrestmanor.com, $135-275 d) is an unlikely find—a French chateau in the middle of the Midwestern prairie. Eight rooms, including six suites, are decorated with lots of chintz and antiques. For something less expensive, try the **Baymont Inn & Suites** (4725 Beckley Rd., 269/979-5400, www.baymontinns.com, $80-129 d), which includes free breakfast, high-speed Internet access, and access to a pool.

Battle Creek offers plenty of dining options, from fast-food establishments to fancier fare. One solid choice is the **Arcadia Brewing Company** (103 W. Michigan Ave., 269/963-9690, www.arcadiaales.com, 11am-9pm Mon.-Thurs., 11am-10pm Fri., noon-10pm Sat., $7-18), a microbrewery that specializes in British-style ales and offers an adjacent restaurant and tavern called TC's Wood-Fired Fare. For hearty all-American cuisine, consider **Finley's American Grill** (140 E. Columbia, 269/968-3938, www.finleys-rcfc.com, 11am-10pm Sun.-Thurs., 11am-11pm Fri.-Sat., $6-17), part of a popular southern Michigan chain, with locations in Jackson, Kalamazoo, and Lansing. If you're in the mood for Italian dishes, stop by **Fazoli's** (5445 Beckley Rd., 269/979-8662, www.fazolis.com, 11am-9pm daily, $6-14), part of a nationwide chain that offers pasta bowls, panini sandwiches, pizzas, and tasty favorites like fettuccine alfredo and meat lasagna.

INFORMATION AND SERVICES

For more information about Battle Creek, contact the **Battle Creek/Calhoun County Convention & Visitors Bureau** (77 E. Michigan Ave., Ste. 100, 269/962-2240, www.battlecreekvisitors.org, 8:30am-5pm Mon.-Fri.). For local news, entertainment, and sports, consult the *Battle Creek Enquirer* (www.battlecreekenquirer.com) or watch **WWMT** (www.wwmt.com), the CBS television affiliate that serves Battle Creek, Kalamazoo, and Grand Rapids.

Battle Creek offers all the services necessary for travelers, including groceries, pharmacies, gas stations, laundries, banks, and post offices. In case of an emergency, dial **911** from any cell or public phone. For medical assistance, consult the **Battle Creek Health System** (300 North Ave., 269/966-8000, www.bchealth.com).

GETTING THERE AND AROUND

Battle Creek is accessible via plane, train, bus, and, naturally, car. The **Kalamazoo/Battle Creek International Airport** (AZO, 5235 Portage Rd., Kalamazoo, 269/388-3668, www.azoairport.com) is situated about 25 miles to the southwest, while the **Capital Region International Airport** (LAN, 4100 Capital City Blvd., Lansing, 517/321-6121, www.flylansing.com) lies roughly 59 miles to the northeast. You can rent a vehicle at both locations, from which it'll take you about 24 minutes from Kalamazoo and an hour from Lansing to reach Battle Creek. In addition, **Amtrak** (800/872-7245, www.amtrak.com), **Greyhound** (269/964-1768 or 800/231-2222, www.greyhound.com), and **Indian Trails** (800/292-3831, www.indiantrails.com) all serve the same station (119 S. McCamly St.) in town.

If you have a car, you can reach Battle Creek via I-94, I-69, and several state highways and county roads. From downtown Detroit, for instance, you can take M-10 North and I-75 South, merge onto I-96 West, continue onto M-14 West and I-94 West, and follow M-66 North to downtown Battle Creek. Once here, you can stick with your car, opt for your feet or a bike, or use **Battle Creek Transit** (269/966-3474, one-way $1.25 adults, $0.60 seniors, free for children shorter than fare box), which offers bus service in and around town.

Kalamazoo and Vicinity

Yes, there really is a city named Kalamazoo. In reference to the area's bubbling natural springs, the name is derived from an Indian word meaning "place where the water boils." Its notoriety came later, when it inspired the Big Band-era song, "I Gotta Gal in Kalamazoo," as well as Carl Sandburg's poem.

From Grand Rapids, Kalamazoo is a straight shot south on US-131. Produce from the nearby vegetable-growing region, pharmaceutical industries, and several papermaking plants form the foundation of the city's diverse economy. Academia provides steady employment, too:

Kalamazoo is home to Western Michigan University and a number of respected private schools, including the academically renowned Kalamazoo College, site of a popular annual Bach festival and internationally known for its K-Plan, which includes international study and required internships.

Kalamazoo's population of approximately 75,100 comprises a sizable gay community, a substantial African American community, a burgeoning alternative music scene, a number of big-city refugees, and an almost even split between liberals and conservatives.

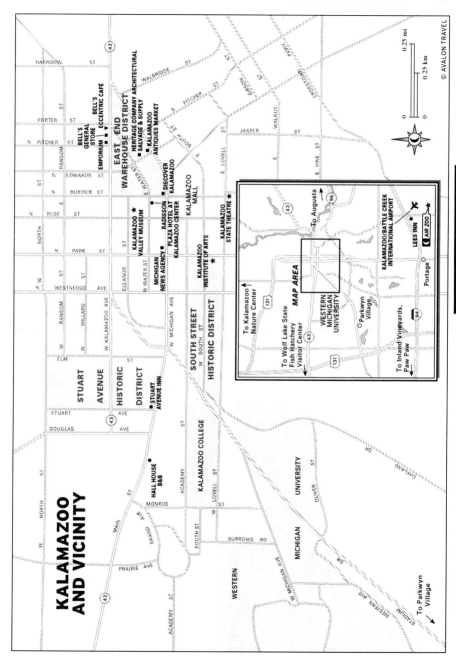

Kalamazoo's balanced economy and population represent such a slice of the American pie that the *Wall Street Journal* featured the city as a focus group during the 1992 presidential election.

While the poet Carl Sandburg didn't think much of Kalamazoo, its downtown streets reveal many of the vanishing pleasures of small-town life: quaint paths perfect for walking, a gracious downtown park, vintage architecture, interesting shops (including a number of antiques outlets), and several top-of-the-line bed-and-breakfasts. There's a great sense of civic pride and an active population that truly gets involved in city affairs. While not really a final destination, Kalamazoo makes a great stop en route to Harbor Country to the south or Lake Michigan's well-known resort communities in the north.

SIGHTS

Built in 1927, the opulent Spanish-style **Kalamazoo State Theatre** (404 S. Burdick St., 269/345-6500, www.kazoostate.com, show times and ticket prices vary) now showcases rock, blues, country, and folk concerts. The interior is a rare example of the work of famed architect John Eberson, who re-created an exotic Mediterranean town with a working cloud machine and stars that really twinkle.

Unlike many other Michigan towns, Kalamazoo experienced few boom-and-bust cycles in the last century, thanks to its plentiful and diversified industry. Houses were well maintained, and many stayed in families for generations. You can see the results of that care in the **South Street Historic District.** Impressive houses went up here between 1847 and World War I, in architectural styles ranging from Greek and Gothic Revival to Georgian and Tudor. Just north of Kalamazoo College, along Stuart and Woodward between West Michigan and North, business owners built large suburban homes in what is now known as the **Stuart Avenue Historic District** to display the wealth they amassed after the Civil War. You'll find a variety of elaborate Queen Anne, Italianate, and Eastlake homes here, including

the meticulously restored **Stuart Avenue Inn** bed-and-breakfast.

If you appreciate Frank Lloyd Wright's architecture, the city's **Parkwyn Village,** at Taliesin and Parkwyn Drives in southwest Kalamazoo, was designed as a cooperative neighborhood by the famed architect in the late 1940s and includes examples of his Usonian style. You can view more Wright homes in the 11000 block of Hawthorne, south of the city of Galesburg.

SHOPPING

Downtown Kalamazoo, which is known as "Central City," offers six distinct shopping districts: Kalamazoo Mall, East End, South Town, Haymarket, Arcadia, and Bronson Park. The streets around the Kalamazoo State Theatre constitute **Kalamazoo Mall** (www.downtownkalamazoo.org), home to coffeehouses, galleries, restaurants, bakeries, and a diverse selection of resale and vintage clothing shops. Stretching from Lovell to Eleanor Streets, it was the first open-air downtown pedestrian mall created by blocking a city street to car traffic. Like many downtown shopping districts, it's suffered from the encroachment of suburban malls, but still offers popular cafés, funky stores that cater to the college crowd, and a gourmet market, among other delights.

If you haven't tired of shopping for antiques in Michigan, head for the **Kalamazoo Antiques Market** (130 N. Edwards St., 269/226-9788), which represents more than 30 quality dealers selling vintage clothing, unique jewelry, vinyl records, pottery, and lots of household stuff. You might also consider the **Emporium** (313 E. Kalamazoo Ave., 269/381-0998, 7pm-9pm Mon.-Fri., 2pm-6pm Sat.-Sun.), worth seeking out for its vintage furniture, despite its unusual hours.

To explore a vintage newsstand, visit the **Michigan News Agency** (308 W. Michigan Ave., 269/343-5958, www.michigannews.biz, 7am-8pm daily), which dates to the 1940s. Inside, you'll find everything from the everyday to the truly eclectic: the usual maps, tobaccos, comics, and newspapers, as well as more than 6,000 magazine titles and 15,000 paperbacks.

The friendly and knowledgeable owners don't seem to mind if you spend the better half of the day perusing their publications. There's also a small selection of books by local writers.

SPORTS AND RECREATION
Spectator Sports
While Kalamazoo might not boast the professional teams of, say, Detroit, sports fans will still find several seasonal options here. If you'd like to catch an IHL hockey game, consider visiting the city October-April, when the **Kalamazoo Wings** (3600 Vanrick Dr., 269/345-1125, www.wingsstadium.com, game times and ticket prices vary) thrash across the ice of Wings Stadium. Of course, if that's not enough, consider the full roster of men's and women's sports at Western Michigan University, where the **WMU Broncos** (1903 W. Michigan Ave., 269/387-8092, www.wmubroncos.com, game times and ticket prices vary) play everything from basketball to soccer to football.

Hiking and Bird-Watching
Nature lovers won't find a much better spot than the **Kalamazoo Nature Center** (7000 N. Westnedge Ave., 269/381-1574, www.naturecenter.org, 9am-5pm Mon.-Sat., 1pm-5pm Sun., $6 adults, $5 seniors 55 and over, $4 children 4-13). At 1,100 acres, it ranks as one of the largest nature centers in the Midwest, with over 11 miles of trails, an arboretum, an herb garden, a restored 1858 homestead housing crafts and local artifacts, and a peaceful glen that was the favorite stomping ground of author James Fenimore Cooper. Other exhibits include a free-flying butterfly zone, an indoor bird-watching area that looks out over the trees and grounds, and a re-created 1830s settlers' farm.

ACCOMMODATIONS
Lee's Inn (2615 Fairfield Rd., 269/382-6100, www.leesinn.com, $77-125 d) is one of the more affordable lodgings in town, with an indoor pool, high-speed wireless Internet access, and a bright, airy breakfast room. For other reasonable deals, Kalamazoo offers a wide assortment of chain hotels and motels, including **Comfort Inn** (739 W. Michigan Ave., 269/384-2800, www.comfortinn.com, $100-145 d), an ideal location for exploring the downtown area.

For a more distinctive experience, consider the ◖ **Stuart Avenue Inn** (229 Stuart Ave., 269/342-0230, www.stuartavenueinn.com, $75-100 d), widely regarded as the city's best B&B. It comprises three adjacent 19th-century homes (including the Bartlett-Upjohn House of pharmaceutical fame) and lovely perennial gardens. The present owners furnished the inn's well-appointed rooms with many of their own antiques as well as goodies collected on shopping sprees around the state. The **Hall House Bed and Breakfast** (106 Thompson St., 269/343-2500, www.hallhouse.com, $109-199 d) offers six rooms in a restored 1923 home. Just steps away from private Kalamazoo College, it's popular with families of students and visiting professors.

FOOD
You can't leave Kalamazoo without stopping by the highly touted ◖ **Bell's Eccentric Café** (355 E. Kalamazoo Ave., 269/382-2332, www.bellsbeer.com, 11am-midnight Mon.-Wed., 11am-1am Thurs.-Sat., noon-midnight Sun., $3-7), part of Bell's Brewery, formerly known as the Kalamazoo Brewing Company, a forerunner of the brewpub craze. Owner Larry Bell's more than 20 acclaimed brews, including Amber Ale, Kalamazoo Stout, and Cherry Stout, have won a loyal following in Chicago, where much of his output is sold. While you're downing a few pints, nibble on some munchies in the smoke-free eatery. This appealing spot has board games scattered around the tables, table tennis, and live acoustic music on Friday and Saturday nights. In warm weather, casual crowds congregate on the outdoor "beer garden" patio.

INFORMATION AND SERVICES
For more information about the Kalamazoo area, contact the **Discover Kalamazoo** (141

THE HEARTLAND

E. Michigan Ave., Ste. 100, 269/488-9000, www.discoverkalamazoo.com, 8am-5pm Mon.-Fri.). For local news, entertainment, and sports, consult the *Kalamazoo Gazette* (www.mlive.com/kzgazette) or watch **WWMT** (www.wwmt.com), the CBS television affiliate that serves Battle Creek, Kalamazoo, and Grand Rapids.

With its assortment of groceries, pharmacies, gas stations, laundries, banks, and other helpful establishments, Kalamazoo can fulfill most travelers' needs. For mailing issues, you'll find over a dozen **post offices** in and around Kalamazoo; visit www.usps.com for locations and hours.

In case of an emergency, dial **911** from any cell or public phone. For medical assistance, consult **Borgess Health** (1521 Gull Rd., 269/226-7000, www.borgess.com).

GETTING THERE AND AROUND

Kalamazoo is accessible via plane, train, bus, and, of course, car. The **Kalamazoo/Battle Creek International Airport** (AZO, 5235 Portage Rd., 269/388-3668, www.azoairport.com), for example, is just south of town; from there, you can hail a taxi or hire a rental car. In addition, **Amtrak** (800/872-7245, www.amtrak.com), **Greyhound** (269/337-8201 or 800/231-2222, www.greyhound.com), and **Indian Trails** (800/292-3831, www.indiantrails.com) all serve the same station (459 N. Burdick St.).

If, however, you've chosen to drive around the state of Michigan, you can easily reach Kalamazoo via I-94, US-131, and several state highways or county roads. From downtown Detroit, for instance, you can take M-10 North and I-75 South, merge onto I-96 West, continue onto M-14 West, and follow I-94 West to Kalamazoo; without traffic, the 143-mile trip should take less than 2.25 hours. From Chicago, meanwhile, you can take I-90 East, merge onto I-94 East, and follow the I-94 East Business Route/US-131 Business Route to Kalamazoo, a 147-mile trip that usually requires about 2.25 hours. Just be advised that,

en route from the Windy City, parts of I-90 East and I-94 East serve as the Indiana Toll Road.

Of course, you can also reach Kalamazoo from Grand Rapids via US-131 South and the US-131 South Business Route; without traffic, this 51-mile journey should take about 49 minutes. Once here, you can simply stick with your car, opt for walking or biking when convenient, or use **Kalamazoo Metro Transit** (269/337-8222, www.kmetro.com, one-way $1.50 adults, $0.75 seniors and children less than 48 inches tall), which provides bus service in and around town.

GREATER KALAMAZOO
🄲 Air Zoo

Just south of the Kalamazoo/Battle Creek International Airport, you'll spy the excellent **Air Zoo** (6151 Portage Rd., 269/382-6555, www.airzoo.org, 9am-5pm Mon.-Sat., noon-5pm Sun., $10 pp). Considered the nation's premier museum of military aircraft, the three-campus Air Zoo stands out because of its emphasis on education. Not only can visitors examine vintage planes, like the Curtiss P-40 Warhawk or Grumman F-14A Tomcat, they can also sit at the controls of state-of-the-art flight simulators and get a small taste of what fighter pilots experience.

This enormous museum also features educational flight-related displays, such as a 2,000-square-foot exhibit chronicling the history of aircraft carriers (complete with over 400 archival photographs and three large models). In addition, the Air Zoo's original facility (now its East Campus) houses the Michigan Space Science Center, a 17,000-square-foot repository of space artifacts, from a Gemini crew-training simulator to a full-size replica of a Mercury space capsule. This impressive facility, much of which was once located near Jackson, offers an interactive exhibit as well. The International Space Station Exhibit uses hands-on demonstrations, simulations, models, theaters, and other experiences to illustrate the history and everyday operations of the largest international peacetime project in the world.

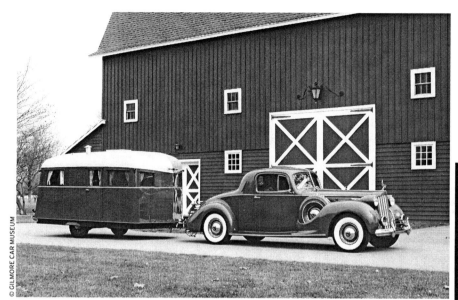

© GILMORE CAR MUSEUM

THE HEARTLAND

Gilmore Car Museum, near Kalamazoo

Gilmore Car Museum

While in the Kalamazoo area, you simply must put aside a few hours for the **Gilmore Car Museum** (6865 Hickory Rd., Hickory Corners, 269/671-5089, www.gilmorecarmuseum.org, 9am-5pm Mon.-Fri., 9am-6pm Sat.-Sun. May-Oct., $12 adults, $11 seniors 62 and over, $9 children 7-15), considered one of the top five car museums in the United States. Situated on 90 landscaped acres northeast of Kalamazoo, not far from Gull Lake, the Gilmore Car Museum houses nearly 200 vintage automobiles in several restored historic barns. Exhibits range from an 1899 locomotive to the infamous 1948 Tucker to muscle cars of the 1970s. Other treats include a new miniature museum and an authentic 1941 diner, a great place for an afternoon snack. All buildings are wheelchair-accessible.

Grand Rapids

Grand Rapids—the state's second-largest city, with a population of 190,400—owes its development and name to the rapids of the free-flowing Grand River, a place of gathering and exchange since Louis Campau established a trading post here in 1826. The power and transportation afforded by the river, coupled with the abundance of wood from the neighboring forests, made the growth of the city's furniture industry a natural.

By 1854, logging had become an important industry, and Grand Rapids entered the most vigorous phase of its development. Huge quantities of logs were floated down the Grand to Grand Rapids' mills. Upstream mill owners, seeing the valuable timber floating unattended

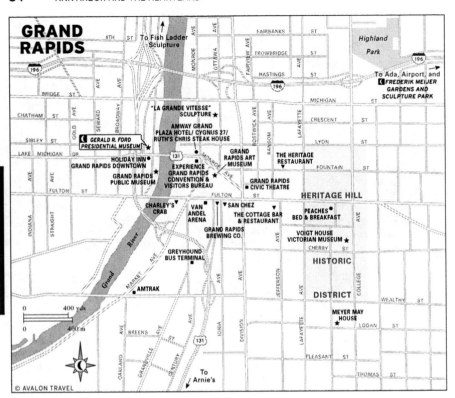

past their mills, often stole the logs and cut them into lumber. This practice, known as "hogging," precipitated fierce brawls along the Flat, Rogue, Grand, and other area rivers and caused the birth of the "river driver," a colorful character who rode the logs downstream to ensure they reached their final destination safely.

Grand Rapids was not always the Calvinist stronghold it is today. During the 1860s, Campau Square was notorious for its brothels, gambling houses, and basement bars. It became better known for its furniture making in 1876, when the city's wares were displayed at America's centennial celebration in Philadelphia. In 1880, the incorporation of the Wolverine Chair and Furniture Company helped solidify that reputation; by 1900, Grand Rapids was nicknamed "Furniture City." The moniker still sticks today, since the area

serves as headquarters for Herman Miller and Steelcase, two of the largest office furniture companies in the country.

Grand Rapids went through a decline in the early 1980s, but somehow managed to reinvent itself as a thriving showcase for the arts, local history, and business. Today, the downtown sparkles with busy hotels, shopping areas, pedestrian malls, and public artworks. One of the most striking downtown sights is Alexander Calder's dramatic sculpture, *La Grande Vitesse,* a 42-ton strawberry-red sculpture that pays homage to the rapids that built the city. Controversial at first, it has since become a symbol of Grand Rapids. More recent city improvements include a new ecofriendly Grand Rapids Public Museum and the addition of one of the nation's largest lion exhibits at the John Ball Zoo.

Much of the redevelopment can be attributed to the area's loyal and exceedingly generous business community, a group that includes the headquarters for the Meijer Corporation (pioneers of the dual grocery/discount store phenomenon) and Amway, that genius of direct marketing, which racks up annual sales in the billions. The names DeVos and Van Andel—the founding families of Amway—seem to top the list of every charitable cause in town. Most of the business and civic leaders are alumni of nearby Holland's Hope College (part of the Reformed Church in America) or of Grand Rapids' Calvin College, run by the Christian Reformed Church. Grand Rapids, by the way, is the epicenter of religious publishing in the United States.

Hardworking Grand Rapids may be known for its Protestant work ethic, but a surprising amount of diversity hides beneath the city's Calvinist veneer. Yes, it's a Republican stronghold, but Grand Rapids is also home to an active alternative press and one of the state's largest Native American populations. The city's older neighborhoods celebrate a mix of cultures, comprising Asian, Latino, African American, Lithuanian, Ukrainian, German, and Polish communities.

SIGHTS
Heritage Hill Historic District
As a manufacturing city with many locally owned businesses, Grand Rapids housed early residents who earned considerable riches and weren't shy about displaying them. Prominent families, including those who owned the city's famed furniture factories, built their mansions on the city's hillside where they could overlook their domain, from far above the smoke and soot their factories generated. **Heritage Hill** (616/459-8950, www.heritage-hillweb.org) was their neighborhood of choice from roughly 1840 through 1920. Located just east of downtown, it displays the wealth of Grand Rapids' lumber boom, with more than 60 architectural styles reflected in its 1,300 residences. Considered the city's first neighborhood, Heritage Hill is now one of

the largest urban historic districts in the country.

As in most of America's urban areas, today's Heritage Hill residents are more economically and racially diverse. The neighborhood is overseen by the Heritage Hill Association, an active group of organizers who work hard at maintaining both their property and the area's sense of community. Among the most spectacular homes are those built by the city's one-time lumber barons, plus a few others designed or inspired by Frank Lloyd Wright.

The highlight has to be the **Meyer May House** (450 Madison Ave., 616/246-4821, www.meyermayhouse.steelcase.com, 10am-1pm Tues. and Thurs., 1pm-4pm Sun., free), an anomaly in this predominantly Victorian neighborhood. It was designed in 1906 by Frank Lloyd Wright for a prominent local clothier, founder of the May's clothing store chain. Vincent Scully, an architectural historian, has called the Meyer May House the most beautifully and completely restored of Wright's Prairie houses. "To come suddenly into that interior . . . is to be wholly caught up and carried along by something rarely experienced: absolute peace, integral order, deep quiet grandeur and calm—all of it achieved in a house of no more than moderate size," he has said. Through the generous funding of Steelcase, the nationally famous Grand Rapids office furniture maker, the house has since been restored to reflect Wright's original organic building concept, with custom-made furniture, art glass, carpets, light fixtures, even linens.

❰ Gerald R. Ford Presidential Museum
The **Gerald R. Ford Presidential Museum** (303 Pearl St. NW, 616/254-0400, www.ford.utexas.edu, 9am-5pm daily, closed on major holidays, $7 adults, $6 seniors, $3 children 6-18) honors Michigan's only native-born president in this triangular building on the west bank of the Grand River. The nation's 38th president—named to the post on August 9, 1974, after the infamous resignation of Richard Nixon—Ford grew up in Grand Rapids and represented the

THE HEARTLAND

© DANIEL MARTONE

Gerald R. Ford Presidential Museum

Fifth Congressional District in Michigan from 1948 to 1973, when he became the nation's vice president.

Renovated in 1997, the museum portrays both the private life and public challenges of Ford, president for just two years. The most popular attraction is the full-size replica of the Oval Office as it looked while Ford was president and the holographic tour of the White House. Other exhibits include a surprisingly moving section on Nixon's resignation and Ford's subsequent pardon, the events surrounding the fall of Saigon, and a multimedia re-creation of 1970s pop culture. Visitors can also see President Ford's burial site.

Other Museums

In 2007, the longstanding **Grand Rapids Art Museum** (GRAM, 101 Monroe Center, 616/831-1000, www.artmuseumgr.org, 10am-5pm Tues.-Thurs. and Sat., 10am-9pm Fri., noon-5pm Sun., $8 adults, $7 seniors and students, $5 children 6-17) was moved from its original spot and reborn within an environmentally friendly building that has been hailed by architectural critics throughout the world. Inside, extensive collections include fine 19th- and 20th-century prints, paintings, photographs, sculptures, and decorative arts with an emphasis on furniture.

The art museum's major competition for the dollars and time of museum-goers is the **Grand Rapids Public Museum** (272 Pearl St. NW, 616/456-3977, www.grmuseum.org, 9am-5pm Mon.-Sat., noon-5pm Sun., closed on major holidays, $8 adults, $3 children 3-17). Arguably the city's best museum, the Public is housed in a spectacular structure and ranks as the largest general museum in the state. It cost $35 million to build in 1995, much of it a gift from Amway cofounder Jay Van Andel.

The Grand Rapids Public Museum holds an outstanding permanent collection of incredible size and scope. Here, you can witness the massive flywheel of a 1905 Corliss-type steam engine that once powered the city's furniture factories in "The Furniture City" exhibit, walk through a re-creation of 1890s Grand Rapids,

© DANIEL MARTONE

Grand Rapids Public Museum

take a turn aboard a restored 1928 Spillman carousel, or see stars at the Roger B. Chaffee Planetarium. The groundbreaking exhibit "Anishinabek: The People of This Place" sensitively explores the culture and artifacts of the Anishinabe people, western Michigan's Native Americans. An illuminating explanation of the state's indigenous Ottawa, Chippewa, and Potawatomi peoples, it includes video interviews that trace the modern challenges of Native Americans and the stereotypes that continue to haunt them.

◖ Frederik Meijer Gardens and Sculpture Park

Another local benefactor—Fred Meijer, owner and founder of the Meijer grocery/discount stores—has given back to his hometown with the spectacular **Frederik Meijer Gardens and Sculpture Park** (1000 E. Beltline Ave. NE, 616/957-1580, www.meijergardens.org, 9am-5pm Mon. and Wed.-Sat., 9am-9pm Tues., noon-5pm Sun., $12 adults, $9 seniors and students, $6 children 5-13, $4 children 3-4), which

opened its doors in 1995. Its 125 acres encompass a 15,000-square-foot tropical conservatory (the state's largest), an outdoor area of colorful flower gardens complemented by ponds, woods, and wetlands, and an extensive collection of sculpture—including works by Auguste Rodin, Henry Moore, Claes Oldenburg, and Coosje van Bruggen. Quotations throughout the gardens by Michigan poets, such as Theodore Roethke and Jim Harrison, connect people to the plants.

THE ARTS

Grand Rapids' performing arts scene is rich and diverse, offering everything from Michigan's only professional ballet company to summertime concerts at the outdoor amphitheater in Frederik Meijer Gardens. One must-see is the **Grand Rapids Civic Theatre** (30 Division Ave., 616/222-6650, www.grct.org, show times and ticket prices vary), which represents a grand piece of the city's architecture. The largest community theater in Grand Rapids and one of the largest in the United States, this impressive

THE MAKING OF A PRESIDENT

Born in Omaha, Nebraska, as Leslie Lynch King Jr., the man who would eventually be known as Gerald R. Ford Jr. (1913-2006), actually spent the first few years of his life, along with his mother, Dorothy Ayer Gardner, at the home of his maternal grandparents in Grand Rapids, Michigan. Before he'd reached the age of three, Ford's mother, who had previously divorced his abusive father in 1913, married a paint salesman named Gerald Rudolff Ford. Never formally adopted, the future president didn't legally change his name to Gerald Rudolph Ford Jr. until 1935.

Raised in Grand Rapids with three half-brothers from his mother's second marriage, Ford seemed to enjoy a solid relationship with both his mother and his stepfather. As a child, he was involved in the Boy Scouts of America, earning the highest rank of Eagle Scout. In fact, he was the only U.S. president to have earned such an honor.

While in Grand Rapids, Ford attended Grand Rapids South High School, where he became a star athlete and the captain of his football team. Attracting the attention of college recruiters, he eventually enrolled as an undergraduate in the University of Michigan, where, as center and linebacker, he helped the Wolverines achieve undefeated seasons and national titles in both 1932 and 1933. Following his graduation in 1935 with a Bachelor of Arts in economics, he accepted an assistant coaching job for the football and boxing teams at Yale University, after which he attended and graduated from Yale Law School.

Over the ensuing decades, he opened a law practice with a friend, enlisted in the U.S. Navy during World War II, married a department store fashion consultant, with whom he had four children, and spent 25 years as a member of the U.S. House of Representatives. Eventually, he replaced Spiro Agnew as vice president in the Nixon presidential administration and, following Nixon's Watergate scandal and subsequent resignation, became the nation's 38th president. During his one presidential term,

landmark offers six main-stage and two children's productions annually in a restored 1903 theater once known as The Majestic.

ACCOMMODATIONS AND FOOD

For one of the best downtown values, consider the **Holiday Inn Grand Rapids Downtown** (310 Pearl St. NW, 616/235-7611, www.holidayinn. com, $102-174 d), centrally located near the Gerald Ford and other public museums, with high-speed Internet access, a pool, a fitness center, a restaurant, and clean, attractive rooms. Pets are allowed.

At the other end of the spectrum, the ◖ **Amway Grand Plaza Hotel** (187 Monroe NW, 616/774-2000, www.amwaygrand.com, $170-275 d) ranks as the finest lodging in Grand Rapids and one of Michigan's top hotels. Two hotels actually make up the complex: the original 1913 Pantlind, and the newer Glass

Tower, completed in 1981. Depending on your mood, you can choose from a lush traditional or cool contemporary room. In all, the two house more than 680 rooms, nine restaurants and coffee shops, several elegant boutiques, and a state-of-the-art fitness center.

The city's oldest operating bar and restaurant, **The Cottage Bar & Restaurant** (18 LaGrave Ave., 616/454-9088, www.cottagebar.biz, 11am-midnight Mon.-Thurs., 11am-12:30am Fri.-Sat., $4-8), concocts Grand Rapids' best burgers and three different styles of chili. The outside café is a popular meeting place in good weather.

Tapas, paella, and other specialties of the Iberian peninsula draw crowds tired of the all-too-common prime rib and pasta to sunny ◖ **San Chez** (38 W. Fulton, 616/774-8272, www.sanchezbistro.com, 11:30am-10pm Mon.-Thurs., 11:30am-11pm Fri., noon-11pm Sat., 4pm-10pm Sun., $4-20). Lively and fun, it he made the controversial decision to pardon Richard Nixon for any crimes that he might have committed against the country during his presidency. In addition, he tried to battle rising inflation, confronted a potential swine flu epidemic, supported the Equal Rights Amendment, officially ended American involvement in the Vietnam War, faced two assassination attempts, and ultimately lost his bid for reelection to Jimmy Carter.

In the years following his presidency, Ford kept fairly busy. He moved with his wife to Denver, Colorado, and, in 1977, established the Gerald R. Ford Institute of Public Policy at Michigan's Albion College. In 1981, he opened the Gerald R. Ford Presidential Library on the North Campus of his alma mater, Ann Arbor's University of Michigan, and established the Gerald R. Ford Presidential Museum in Grand Rapids. By 1988, he was a member of several corporate boards, and in 2001, he received the John F. Kennedy Profiles in Courage Award for his controversial decision to pardon Richard Nixon in order to heal the nation following the

Watergate scandal. That was the same year that he broke from the Republican Party by supporting equal treatment of gay and lesbian couples.

Five years later, at the age of 93, President Ford died at his home in Rancho Mirage, California, having become the longest-lived U.S. President, being 45 days older than Ronald Reagan was when he passed away. He also had the distinction of being the only person ever to hold the presidential office without being elected as president or vice president. Of course, despite his rocky road as president, he was considered by many to be an honest, kind-hearted, likable "everyman," no doubt a hallmark of his Midwestern roots. It's no wonder, then, that Grand Rapids citizens are generally proud of their native son – and perhaps it explains why several sites in and around Grand Rapids bear his name, including the Gerald R. Ford Middle School, the Gerald R. Ford International Airport, and the Gerald R. Ford Freeway, the stretch of I-196 that passes through Allegan, Ottawa, and Kent Counties.

THE HEARTLAND

draws an eclectic crowd with entrées such as spiced Moroccan meatballs and lamb ribs with raspberry chili sauce.

Charley's Crab (63 Market Ave. SW, 616/459-2500, www.muer.com, 11:30am-4pm and 4:30pm-10pm Mon.-Thurs., 11:30am-4pm and 4:30pm-11pm Fri., 4:30pm-11pm Sat., 10am-9pm Sun., $12-35) is part of Chuck Muer's well-loved, nationwide chain of seafood restaurants. Try one of the fresh catches or one of the always-tasty pastas, or load up on carbs at the Sunday brunch. The signature rolls have been copied by a number of restaurants across the state. In good weather, ask for an outside table overlooking the Grand River.

INFORMATION AND SERVICES

For more information about the Grand Rapids area, contact the **Experience Grand Rapids Convention & Visitors Bureau** (171 Monroe

Ave. NW, Ste. 700, 616/459-8287, www.visitgrandrapids.org, 9am-5pm Mon.-Fri.) or the **Grand Rapids Area Chamber of Commerce** (111 Pearl St. NW, 616/771-0300, www.grandrapids.org, 8:30am-5pm Mon.-Fri.). For official city-related information, visit www.grand-rapids.mi.us. For local news, entertainment, and sports, consult the **Grand Rapids Press** (www.mlive.com/grpress) or watch **WOOD** (www.woodtv.com), the NBC television affiliate.

Grand Rapids offers all the services you might require, including gas stations, laundries, and banks. For groceries, prescriptions, and other supplies, stop by a **Meijer** superstore (www.meijer.com); there are several in the area. For mailing needs, you'll find over a dozen **post offices** in and around Grand Rapids; visit www.usps.com for locations and hours.

In case of an emergency, dial **911** from any cell or public phone. For medical assistance, consult **Spectrum Health** (866/989-7999, www.spectrum-health.org), which oversees several hospitals and medical centers in the region.

GETTING THERE AND AROUND

As with several other towns in the Heartland, Grand Rapids is accessible via plane, train, bus, and, naturally, car. **Gerald R. Ford International Airport** (GRR, 5500 44th St. SE, 616/233-6000, www.grr.org), for instance, lies southeast of town; from there, you can hire a rental car via Avis, Budget, and other national chains or opt for a luxury sedan from **Metro Cars** (616/827-6700 or 800/456-1701, www. metrocars.com), which offers 24-hour dispatch service from the airports in both Detroit and Grand Rapids. Typically, a ride from the Ford airport to downtown Grand Rapids will cost about $40. Meanwhile, **Amtrak** (431 Wealthy St. SW, 800/872-7245, www.amtrak.com) also serves the city. In addition, it's also possible to reach Grand Rapids by bus; **Greyhound** (616/456-1700 or 800/231-2222, www.greyhound.com) and **Indian Trails** (800/292-3831, www.indiantrails.com) both provide service to the same station (250 Grandville Ave. SW).

Of course, if you've chosen to drive around the state of Michigan, you can also reach Grand Rapids via I-96, I-196, US-131, and several state highways and county roads. From downtown Detroit, for instance, you can take M-10 North, merge onto I-696 West, continue onto I-96 West, and follow I-196 West to Grand Rapids; without traffic, the 158-mile trip should take around 2.25 hours. From Chicago, meanwhile, you can take I-90 East, merge onto I-94 East, and follow I-196 North and I-196 East, a 178-mile trip that usually requires about 2.75 hours. Just be advised that, en route from the Windy City, parts of I-90 East and I-94 East serve as the Indiana Toll Road.

Once in Grand Rapids, Michigan's second-largest city, you'll probably want to stick with your car to get around. If you're tired of driving, though, you can almost always hop aboard **The Rapid** (616/776-1100, www.ridetherapid. org, one-way $1.50 adults, $0.75 seniors, children under 42 inches free), an outstanding public transit system that even links Grand Rapids to surrounding towns, from Wyoming to Grandville.

Lansing and East Lansing

In the 1940s, the WPA *Guide to Michigan* described Lansing as a place where "the political activity of a state capital, the rumbling tempo of an industrial city, and the even temper of a farming community are curiously blended." Over 70 years later, it's still an apt description.

Curiously, Lansing was developed by a legislative prank. Until 1847, Detroit was the state's capital, as mandated in a provision in the 1835 constitution. When the provision expired, legislators (two of whom had been burned in effigy by Detroit rowdies) decided that the Detroit border was in constant danger of invasion and voted to move the capital. Where to put it, however, posed a problem. After months of wrangling and debating just

about every settlement in lower Michigan, someone jokingly suggested Lansing, a wide spot in the road that consisted of one log house and a sawmill. Amid laughs and for want of a better solution, it won the vote. The state's seat of government was moved in 1847.

Even the name was a lark. The original settlement was named after Lansing, New York, and a New York chancellor. When it became the new capital, many wanted to rename the tiny town Michigan or Michigamme. But the legislature once again became bogged down in political infighting. Lansing it remained.

Once the decision was made and the place had a name, it began to grow. By the time the

© 123RF.COM

the state capitol building in Lansing

THE HEARTLAND

city was incorporated in 1859, it had 4,000 residents, a number of small businesses, a new capitol building, and two newspapers to cover it all. The city received another economic boost in the early 1900s, when R. E. Olds began making his "merry Oldsmobile" here.

Today, Lansing is the state's governmental seat, headquarters for many trade and professional associations, and home to heavy industry. East Lansing, a neighboring community that is part of the capital city in all respects except government, is the home of Michigan State University, part of the Big Ten conference. Ironically, the powers-that-be also selected the university site by default.

Urban decay and rampant freeway construction have bruised downtown Lansing, and the city is often all but empty after five o'clock. While it has been described as a city in search of a center, it has a surprising amount to offer once you find it: good museums, a full plate of MSU events, some of the state's loveliest and most accessible gardens, and even a minor league baseball team, the Lansing Lugnuts.

SIGHTS
◖ Michigan State University

Dubbed "Moo U," Michigan State University was established in 1855 as the country's first agricultural college and the forerunner of the nationwide land-grant university system. Despite its nicknames and rather well-known reputation as a party school, the campus has a long, rich history and an excellent reputation in many fields of study—especially agricultural ones, of course. Credit for its founding goes to a group of enlightened Michigan farmers who began lobbying in 1849 for a state college to promote modern agriculture. They chose the 677 acres of forest five miles east of the new state capital, in part because they wanted the school to be autonomous and not tied to an existing university.

Today, the MSU campus has grown to more than 5,000 beautifully landscaped acres, home to more than 7,000 different species and varieties of trees, shrubs, and vines. In the older part of the campus, curving drives and Gothic buildings create a park-like setting, shaded by

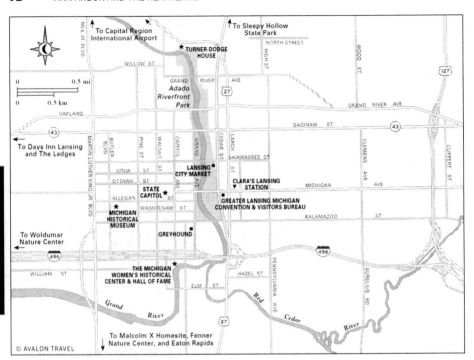

huge beeches and some gnarled white oaks that date back more than 200 years. Students walk to class through what has become a true arboretum with the passing of time, home to more than 5,000 varieties of woodsy plants and trees.

The campus has long been regarded as one giant outdoor laboratory. Very few planted environments in the Midwest have enjoyed such sustained commitment for more than 150 years. At one point, a school policy expected three hours per day of manual labor from all students, part of the hands-on laboratory approach that helped the university maintain the campus and also enabled poor students to afford a college education. Today, both students and professional landscapers maintain the university's impressive collection of gardens.

Campus Gardens

Among MSU's extensive plantings are the **Horticulture Gardens** (B-110 Plant and Soil Sciences Building, 517/353-3770, www.hrt. msu.edu/our-gardens, sunrise-sunset daily, free). The gardens are responsible for transforming a bleak-looking, post-1960 section of campus into a dramatic environment. Once as flat and bare as the newest subdivision, the 14-acre area is now full of pergolas, gazebos, arbors, and topiary. The entrance is off Bogue Street, south of Wilson Road, not far from the Wharton Center. Before venturing into the gardens, pick up a map at the Plant and Soil Sciences Building.

South of the Horticulture Gardens is the year-round **Clarence E. Lewis Landscape Arboretum** (517/355-5191, www.hrt.msu.edu, sunrise-sunset daily, free), dedicated in 1984 as an instructional arboretum for students interested in landscape development. The ever-growing collection of demonstration gardens experiment with vegetables, fruit, herbs, conifers, and native plants. You'll also be able

LANSING AND MSU CAMPUS

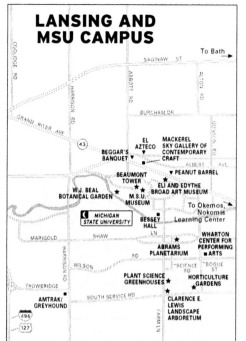

has been called one of the Midwest's best-kept secrets. In 2001, Michigan's leading public natural and cultural history museum also became the state's first museum to receive Smithsonian affiliate status. Three floors of exhibits concentrate on the history of the Great Lakes region; on display are numerous tools, quilts, folk art pieces, and other archaeological artifacts. Popular stops include the fur-trader's cabin and the life-size dinosaur dioramas.

Also on campus, at the intersection of Auditorium and Physics Roads, the relatively new **Eli and Edythe Broad Art Museum** (547 E. Circle Dr., 517/884-3900, www.broadmuseum.msu.edu, 10am-5pm Tues.-Thurs. and Sat.-Sun., noon-9pm Fri., closed on major holidays, free), which has inherited an impressive array of artwork from Kresge Art Museum, which closed in 2012, now houses a permanent collection that spans numerous centuries from the ancient Greek and Roman periods to the contemporary era. Designed by award-winning architect Zaha Hadid, the dynamic glass-and-steel edifice contains thousands of works of art, from Greek and Roman antiquities to Renaissance illuminations to 20th-century sculptures from artists like Alexander Calder and Jenny Holzer. Wide-ranging highlights include a dramatic *Vision of St. Anthony of Padua* by Francisco Zurburán, Andy Warhol's *Marilyn*, and a solid collection of art from the 1960s and 1970s, an era often overlooked by other museums. In keeping with the mission of the museum, future acquisitions will likely focus on other modern and contemporary works from 1945-present.

Other Museums

Part of the huge Michigan Library and Historical Center, the **Michigan Historical Museum** (702 W. Kalamazoo St., 517/373-3559, www.michigan.gov/museum, 9am-4:30pm Mon.-Fri., 10am-4pm Sat., 1pm-5pm Sun., free) has become a pilgrimage for many history buffs. With three floors and more than 30 permanent galleries, it tells a detailed story of Michigan's rise from wilderness to industrial powerhouse. Unlike at

to walk through a water garden, a sculpture garden, a Japanese garden, and a topiary garden, among other displays. Another campus area worth a special stop is the **W. J. Beal Botanical Garden** (www.cpa.msu.edu/beal), founded in 1873 and believed to be the oldest continuously operated garden of its type in the country. Situated between the Red Cedar River and West Circle Drive, this outdoor museum of living plants includes more than 2,000 species arranged by family and economic use, as well as exotic flowering landscape specimens and an enlightening section on endangered plants.

Campus Museums

With a collection of more than one million items, the 150-year-old **Michigan State University Museum** (W. Circle Dr., 517/355-7474, www.museum.msu.edu, 9am-5pm Mon.-Fri., 10am-5pm Sat., 1pm-5pm Sun., donation suggested), situated east of Beaumont Tower,

THE HEARTLAND

© GREATER LANSING CVB

a packed Spartan football game at MSU

many self-serving state museums, however, the narrative here is frank and intelligent. Placards explain how within a few generations of contact with European settlers, the state's Native American cultures transformed from self-sufficient lifestyles to those with a dependence on manufactured goods. The museum also contains an excellent and detailed copper-mining exhibit that's probably better than any found in the U.P. today. It features a walk-through copper mine and videos on life in the mining camps.

The 3rd floor chronicles more recent history, including the dawn of the automobile age and the Great Depression. On the lower level, a small but choice museum store offers lighthouse prints, jewelry crafted from Petoskey stones, and one of the state's best selections of books relating to the history of African Americans. The Michigan Library and Historical Center complex also houses the state archives and state library, a popular pilgrimage spot for genealogists from around the country. The building itself is of interest, too, designed by prominent Detroit architect William Kessler, who relied largely on native building materials.

Not far from downtown Lansing, **The Michigan Women's Historical Center & Hall of Fame** (213 W. Main St., 517/484-1880, www.michiganwomenshalloffame.org, noon-5pm Wed.-Fri., noon-4pm Sat., 2pm-4pm Sun., $2.50 adults, $2 seniors, $1 children 5-18) honors the mostly unsung achievements of the state's native daughters through changing and permanent exhibitions. It celebrates the lives and contributions of Michigan women such as Sojourner Truth, a former slave and crusader for human rights; Laura Smith Haviland, an organizer of one of the state's first Underground Railroad stations; Anne Howard Shaw, a minister and physician whose dynamic leadership resulted in the passage of the 19th Amendment; and Gilda Radner, a courageous Detroit-born actress and comedienne.

Adado Riverfront Park

Lansing's Louis F. Adado Riverfront Park and Trail System ranks as one of the finest urban green spaces in the state. This greenbelt stretches on both sides of the Grand River from Kalamazoo Avenue just north of I-496 to North Street, three miles downstream. A riverwalk, popular with joggers and in-line skaters, runs along the entire east side of the river.

FAMOUS SPARTANS AND WOLVERINES

Established during the 19th century, both Michigan State University (MSU) and the University of Michigan (UM) have long, rich histories, with an even longer list of attendees and graduates. Here are just some of their more notable alumni:

FORMER MSU SPARTANS

- James Caan, actor
- Jim Cash, screenwriter
- John Engler, Michigan governor
- Jim Harrison, poet/novelist/essayist
- Earvin "Magic" Johnson, NBA player
- Sam Raimi, screenwriter/director/producer
- Robert Urich, actor
- Timothy Zahn, science fiction writer

FORMER UM WOLVERINES

- Selma Blair, actress
- Tom Brady, NFL quarterback
- Gerald R. Ford, U.S. president
- David Alan Grier, actor/comedian
- James Earl Jones, actor
- Lawrence Kasdan, screenwriter/director/producer
- Christine Lahti, actress
- Lucy Liu, actress
- Madonna, singer/actress
- Arthur Miller, playwright/essayist
- Susan Orlean, journalist
- David Paymer, actor/director
- Gilda Radner, actress/comedienne
- Mike Wallace, journalist/media personality

ENTERTAINMENT
Nightlife
East Lansing's best club is arguably **Rick's American Café** (224 Abbot Rd., 517/351-2288, www.ricksamericancafe.com, 6:30pm-close Mon.-Sat., 8pm-close Sun., cover charges vary), with great live acts, top-notch DJs, and drink specials every night. Things tend to get loud, so be prepared. **The Green Door Blues Bar & Grill** (2005 E. Michigan Ave., 517/482-6376, www. greendoorlive.com, 3pm-2am Mon.-Sat., 7pm-2am Sun., no cover) features some top-notch jazz and blues acts and dynamite drink specials, while offering the kind of moody lounge atmosphere you might find in a bigger city.

The Arts
BoarsHead Theater (425 S. Grand Ave., 517/484-7805, www.boarshead.org, show times and ticket prices vary), central Michigan's oldest professional theater, offers a season of dynamic productions at the city's Center for the Arts. This talented troupe performs October-May, and tries especially hard to make theater accessible to everyone.

Lovers of Broadway musicals, dance, comedy routines, and other special events can get their fill at the **Wharton Center for Performing Arts** (517/353-1982, www.whartoncenter.com, show times and ticket prices vary) on the MSU campus. This renowned venue boasts four unique stages—the Pasant Theatre, the MSU Concert Auditorium, the Fairchild Theatre, and Cobb Great Hall, where the Lansing Symphony Orchestra regularly performs.

SHOPPING
Not far from Adado Riverfront Park is the **Lansing City Market** (333 N. Cedar St., 517/483-7460, www.lansingcitymarket.com, 9am-6pm Tues. and Thurs.-Fri., 8am-5pm Sat.). Established in 1909 and relocated to its current spot in 1938, this year-round market attracts plenty of vendors offering fruit,

THE HEARTLAND

© GREATER LANSING CVB

Lansing's Michigan Historical Museum

vegetables, sandwiches, baked goods, and more. After making your purchases, eat at a picnic area near the river.

SPORTS AND RECREATION
Spectator Sports

MSU has a spectator sport for everyone, from football to basketball, hockey to baseball. For scheduling and ticket information on Spartan sporting events, contact the **MSU Athletic Ticket Office** (Jenison Field House, 517/355-1610, www.msuspartans.com, 10am-6pm Mon.-Fri. Aug.-Apr., 10am-5pm Mon.-Fri. May-July).

Golf

Although northern Michigan boasts even more award-winning golf courses, the Heartland has its share of eye-catchers. **Eagle Eye Golf Club** (15500 Chandler Rd., Bath, 517/641-4570, www.hawkhollow.com, daily Apr.-Oct., $40-65 pp) is one such place, located about 10 miles northeast of Lansing on I-69. Even better, this exceptional course is part of a spread that includes three others: the 9-hole Falcon,

the 27-hole Hawk Hollow, and the Little Hawk putting course.

ACCOMMODATIONS AND FOOD

There's no lack of lodgings in the Lansing area, thanks to Big Ten fans and business travelers. You'll find a long list of reliable franchise options, including the **Hampton Inn** (525 N. Canal Rd., 517/627-8381, www.hamptoninn. com, $69-129 d), with well-maintained rooms and a free breakfast bar—an affordable spot for your football-weekend accommodations. For a bit more luxury, try the **Kellogg Hotel & Conference Center** (55 S. Harrison Rd., East Lansing, 517/432-4000, www.kelloggcenter. com, $114-369 d), the only four-star hotel on MSU's campus.

Housed in a restored Victorian-style train station, **Clara's Lansing Station** (637 E. Michigan Ave., 517/372-7120, www.claras.com, 11am-10pm Mon.-Thurs., 11am-midnight Fri.-Sat., 10am-10pm Sun., $9-24) is chock-full of vintage memorabilia, from old train schedules to antique sheet music. The enormous menu is equally eclectic, with a full range of salads, sandwiches, pizzas, pastas, hefty entrées, and ice cream drinks. If you're in the mood for seafood, check out **Mitchell's Fish Market** (2975 Preyde Blvd., 517/482-3474, www.mitchellsfishmarket.com, 11:30am-10pm Mon.-Thurs., 11:30am-11pm Fri.-Sat., 11:30am-9pm Sun., $15-32), where you'll find everything from exotic seafood to local catches.

You can't beat the combination of good burgers, friendly service, inexpensive prices, and cold beer at ◖ **Peanut Barrel** (521 E. Grand River, East Lansing, 517/351-0608, www.peanutbarrel.com, 10am-midnight daily, $4-6). The olive burger is simply to die for. For some good ol' Mexican cuisine, stop by **El Azteco** (225 Ann St., East Lansing, 517/351-9111, www.elazteco.me, 11am-midnight Tues.-Sat., 11am-11pm Sun.-Mon., $5-12), where the atmosphere isn't as dank as it once was, but the food still screams of fine dive cuisine.

INFORMATION AND SERVICES

For more information about Lansing and East Lansing, contact the **Greater Lansing Michigan Convention & Visitors Bureau** (1223 Turner St., Ste. 200, 888/252-6746, www.lansing.org, 8:30am-5pm Mon.-Fri.). For official city-related information, visit www.lansingmi.gov. For local news, entertainment, and sports, consult the *Lansing State Journal* (www.lansingstatejournal.com) or watch **WLNS** (www.wlns.com), the CBS television affiliate that serves Lansing and Jackson.

Between Lansing and East Lansing, you'll surely find everything you need during your trip, from gas stations to banks. For groceries, prescriptions, and other supplies, stop by a **Meijer** superstore (www.meijer.com); there are several in the area. For mailing needs, you'll find over a dozen **post offices** in the Lansing/East Lansing area; visit www.usps.com for locations and hours.

In case of an emergency, dial **911** from any cell or public phone. For medical services, stop by **Sparrow Hospital** (1215 E. Michigan Ave., 517/364-1000, www.sparrow.org).

GETTING THERE AND AROUND

To reach Lansing, travelers can fly into the **Capital Region International Airport** (LAN, 4100 Capital City Blvd., 517/321-6121, www.flylansing.com), where it's possible to hire a taxi or rent a car from one of four different rental agencies. You can also access the Lansing area by taking an **Amtrak** train (800/872-7245, www.amtrak.com) or **Greyhound** bus (517/332-2595 or 800/231-2222, www.greyhound.com) to the East Lansing station (1240 S. Harrison Rd.). There's an additional Greyhound station in Lansing (420 S. Grand Ave., 517/482-4246), which also serves as a regular stop for **Indian Trails** (800/292-3831, www.indiantrails.com).

Of course, if you're headed to Lansing and East Lansing via car, you'll be delighted to know that, given its centralized location in the Lower Peninsula's southern half, you can easily access the capital via I-69, I-96, US-127, and several state highways and county roads. From downtown Detroit, for instance, you can take M-10 North, merge onto I-696 West, continue onto I-96 West, and follow I-496 West to downtown Lansing; without traffic, the 91-mile trip should take around 80 minutes. From Chicago, meanwhile, you can take I-90 East, merge onto I-94 East, continue onto I-69 North, and follow I-496 East, a 218-mile trip that usually requires about 3.25 hours. Just be advised that, en route from the Windy City, parts of I-90 East and I-94 East serve as the Indiana Toll Road.

Once in Lansing, Michigan's capital city and one of the state's largest towns, you'll probably want to navigate the area via car. If you're tired of driving, though, simply hop aboard a bus operated by the well-regarded **Capital Area Transportation Authority** (CATA, 517/394-1000, www.cata.org, one-way $1.25-2.50 adults, children under 42 inches free). As with most capital cities and college towns, however, Lansing and East Lansing also have several reliable cab companies. One such option is **Spartan Cab/Yellow Cab** (517/482-1444, www.capitoltransport.com), which offers 24-hour service every day of the year.

Mount Pleasant

As exemplified by the city seal, Mount Pleasant's history was indelibly shaped by four elements—its Native American heritage as well as agriculture, education, and the discovery of oil. Native Americans, who had been promised lands in an 1855 treaty, began settling within Isabella County the following year. When a timber scout named David Ward purchased the land on the southern side of the Chippewa River, directly opposite what is today the Isabella Indian Reservation, he decided to call the fledgling village Mount Pleasant. Soon, merchants, artisans, and farmers flocked to the area.

The town gradually expanded, and by 1892, there was even a community college, the Central Michigan Normal School and Business Institute, which would eventually become today's Central Michigan University. The discovery of oil in 1928 changed the fortunes of the burgeoning town, which soon boasted hotels, restaurants, oil companies, and plenty of new residents. During the oil boom, many other industries left the area, but oil production kept Mount Pleasant from becoming a ghost town.

Today, Mount Pleasant (with a population of 26,180) is a more laid-back town, celebrated for its rich Chippewa heritage. Its two biggest attractions are, in fact, an Indian-owned casino and an annual powwow. Of course, the area's numerous golf courses, military memorials, recreational parks, and CMU football games also entice visitors.

ZIIBIWING CENTER

The Midwest's premier Native American museum, the **Ziibiwing Center of Anishinabe Culture & Lifeways** (6650 E. Broadway, 989/775-4750, www.sagchip.org/ziibiwing, 10am-6pm Mon.-Sat., $6.50 adults, $3.75 seniors 60 and over and children 5-17) demonstrates the rich culture and history of the Great Lakes' Anishinabe tribe. The permanent "Diba Jimooyung" exhibit illustrates the amazing history of the original inhabitants of the Great Lakes, including their prophecies and their struggle to preserve their land, language, and culture. At different times during the year, the museum often hosts traveling exhibits about tribes from other parts of Michigan and elsewhere in the United States.

ENTERTAINMENT AND EVENTS

⟨ Soaring Eagle Casino and Resort

You might not think that one of the Midwest's largest casinos would be situated in the Mount Pleasant area—instead of in a more tourist-centric place along the coast—but it might make more sense when you consider that the Indian-owned **Soaring Eagle Casino and Resort** (6800 Soaring Eagle Blvd., 888/732-4537, www.soaringeaglecasino.com, 24 hours daily, prices vary) is located next to the state's largest Native American reservation, the Isabella Indian Reservation, home to the Saginaw Chippewa tribe. With its enormous gaming area, six restaurants, and more than 500 well-appointed rooms, the resort can pack in a ton of partygoers at any given moment. Even if you don't like gaming, you can still relax in one of the on-site pools or spend the day at the spa. After dining in one of the resort's eateries or fine restaurants, catch a show at the concert hall, where big-name entertainment often takes to the stage.

⟨ Saginaw Chippewa Tribal Powwow

For over 20 years, the annual **Saginaw Chippewa Tribal Powwow** (7070 E. Broadway, 989/775-4000, www.sagchip.org, free) has offered visitors the opportunity to observe and experience traditional Native American dress, dancing, drumming, chanting, cuisine, and crafts. The competition, held in early August, attracts performers from all over the United

THE HEARTLAND

© MOUNT PLEASANT AREA CVB

an exhibit at the Ziibiwing Center of Anishinabe Culture & Lifeways

States, making it one of the biggest events in the Indian Nation—and a terrific place for outsiders to learn about Native American culture.

SPORTS AND RECREATION
College Sports
Throughout the year, the Central Michigan University Chippewas stage a wide range of sporting events, from football to women's basketball. If you're interested in catching a game while you're in Mount Pleasant, contact the **CMU Athletics Ticket Office** (989/774-3045, www.cmuchippewas.com).

Golf
The Mount Pleasant area offers several decent golf courses. Two options include **Bucks Run Golf Club** (1559 S. Chippewa Rd., 989/773-6830, www.bucksrun.com, daily Apr.-Nov., $30-85 pp w/cart), situated on 290 gorgeous acres that include wetlands, three lakes, and the Chippewa River, and **Riverwood Resort** (1313 E. Broomfield Rd., 989/772-5726, www.riverwoodresort.com, daily Apr.-Oct., $12-48

pp), which offers 27 classic holes, a spacious clubhouse, several deluxe villas, and two dozen bowling lanes.

ACCOMMODATIONS AND FOOD
If you're looking for lodgings beyond the casino, check out **The Green Suites** (5665 E. Pickard Rd., 989/772-2905, www.greensuites.co, $140-200 d), Mount Pleasant's only all-suite hotel. With its proximity to the Soaring Eagle Resort and several nearby golf courses, it's an ideal spot for those visiting the Mount Pleasant area. Suites range in size, from 995-square-foot one-bedroom suites to spacious 1,687-square-foot chambers, but all contain a living room, a dining area, and a kitchen.

The Soaring Eagle Casino isn't the only game in town for food either. **The Brass Cafe and Saloon** (128 S. Main St., 989/772-0864, www.thebrasscafe.com, 11am-10pm Tues.-Sat., $8-16) offers a wide range of menu choices, featuring innovative American and global cuisine. Set within two turn-of-the-20th-century shopfronts, this popular eatery offers an intimate setting for relaxing after a hard day of golf or gambling.

INFORMATION AND SERVICES

For more information about Mount Pleasant, consult the **Mount Pleasant Area Convention & Visitors Bureau** (114 E. Broadway, 989/772-4433, www.mountpleasantwow.com, 8am-5pm Mon.-Fri.). For local and regional news, consult the *Morning Sun* (www.themorningsun.com).

Mount Pleasant might not be as large as other Heartland cities, but it still has its share of groceries, banks, gas stations, and the like. In fact, there's a **Meijer** superstore (www.meijer.com) and a **post office** (www.usps.com) at the same location (1015 E. Pickard St., 989/772-4700).

In case of an emergency, dial **911** from any phone. For medical services, head to **Central Michigan Community Hospital** (1221 South Dr., 989/772-6700, www.cmch.org).

GETTING THERE AND AROUND

To reach Mount Pleasant, which is conveniently situated in the middle of the Lower Peninsula, visitors can fly into **MBS International Airport** (MBS, 8500 Garfield Rd., Freeland, 989/695-5555, www.mbsairport.org), where it's possible to rent a car from one of five national rental agencies. From there, you can then take US-10 West and continue onto M-20 West, toward Mount Pleasant; the 39-mile trip will take about 50 minutes. **Greyhound** (989/772-4246

or 800/231-2222, www.greyhound.com) and **Indian Trails** (800/292-3831, www.indiantrails.com), meanwhile, also offer bus service to the area (300 W. Broomfield St.).

Of course, most folks will likely be driving from elsewhere in Michigan. Luckily, M-20 and US-127 pass directly through the Mount Pleasant area. So, it's a relative snap to reach Mount Pleasant from a variety of destinations. From Lansing, for instance, you can simply take I-496 East, merge onto US-127 North, and take the US-127 Business Route to Mount Pleasant, a 70-mile trip that normally takes a little over an hour. From downtown Detroit, meanwhile, you can take I-375 North, continue onto I-75 North, merge onto US-10 West, and follow M-20 West to Mount Pleasant; without traffic, this 155-mile trip should require less than 2.5 hours. If you're headed from northern Michigan, it's also easy to access Mount Pleasant. From Traverse City, for example, just take South Garfield Avenue, Voice Road, and Clark Road to M-113 East, turn right onto US-131 South and continue toward M-115 East, merge onto US-10 East, and follow US-127 South to Mount Pleasant; without traffic, the 112-mile trip will take roughly two hours. Once here, you can either drive around town or hop aboard one of the buses provided by the **Isabella County Transportation Commission** (ICTC, 2100 E. Transportation Dr., 989/772-9441 or 989/773-2913, one-way $2 adults, $1.50 children under 18, $1 seniors 60 and over), on which the students and faculty members of Central Michigan University greatly depend.

Midland

When the lumbermen withdrew from Midland to follow the green frontier north, the city might have become just another ghost town if it weren't for Herbert H. Dow. In 1890, Dow began a series of experiments to extract chemicals from the common salt brine that was below the surface of most of central Michigan, eventually founding Dow Chemical Company.

Although the 24-year-old was called "Crazy Dow" by the locals when he arrived in town with little but a good idea, he was a surprisingly farsighted inventor and humanitarian who founded a well-planned city of neat streets and good architecture. Today, this city of 42,000 continues to benefit from Dow's influence, and many of the city's attractions—from sports to cultural activities—bear his fingerprints.

SIGHTS

If your schedule's tight, and you have time for only one attraction in Midland, make it the **Dow Gardens** (1809 Eastman Ave., 800/362-4874, www.dowgardens.org, 9am-8:30pm daily mid-Apr.-Labor Day, 9am-6:30pm daily Labor Day-Oct., 9am-4:15pm daily Nov.-mid-Apr., $7 adults, $1 children 6-17) and the buildings designed by Alden B. Dow, Herbert's son. Alden Dow was one of Frank Lloyd Wright's original Taliesin fellows, and

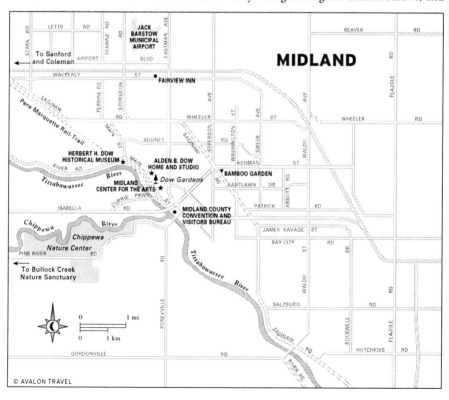

© MIDLAND COUNTY CVB

Alden Dow's home and studio, nestled beside the Dow Gardens

he had a long and distinguished architectural career. Like Wright, he tried to merge architecture and nature, insisting that "gardens never end and buildings never begin."

Developed by Herbert and Alden Dow over the course of more than 70 years, the garden's lovely landscape began as Herbert Dow's extended 10-acre backyard. When he arrived in Midland, the town was a barren landscape of sad stumps left behind by the lumber industry. In 1899, Dow began to landscape the space around his house to show his fellow townsfolk what they could do with their yards. He took his hobby seriously, and corresponded with Luther Burbank and other leading horticulturists of his era. During his lifetime, Dow planted 5,000 fruit trees, including 40 varieties of plums.

Unlike other historic American gardens, which owe a design debt to the formal gardens of Europe, the Dow Gardens are original, an unusual place of unfolding environments often likened to Japanese or Oriental styles. Always an enthusiastic traveler, Dow traveled to Japan frequently and became friends with a noted designer of Tokyo parks.

Texture, form, and contrast are as important here as more obvious displays of blooms. The gardens were renovated in the 1970s by Alden Dow as a retirement project, and more than a thousand trees and shrubs were added. Fantasy environments, including a jungle walk and a yew maze, reveal Dow's gentle, playful spirit. Don't miss the wheelchair-accessible sensory trail, the herb garden, and the extensive garden of perennials.

The **Midland Center for the Arts** (MCFTA, 1801 W. St. Andrews Rd., 989/631-5930, www.mcfta.org, hours and prices vary daily depending on venue and event) is another Alden Dow building. Inside the anthropomorphic, Guggenheim-style structure are two museums, two performance venues, several art studios and lecture halls, and the Saints & Sinners Lounge, a popular hangout before and after concerts and plays. Although there's a lot to see and do at the MCFTA, families favor the **Alden B. Dow Museum of Science and Art**

(10am-4pm Tues.-Wed. and Fri.-Sat., 10am-8pm Thurs. June-Aug., 10am-4pm Wed., Fri., and Sat., 10am-8pm Thurs., 1pm-5pm Sun. Sept.-May, $9 adults, $6 children 4-14, children under 4 free), which features rotating art and science exhibits, a hands-on Hall of Ideas, and a ferocious-looking mastodon that's especially popular with kids.

RECREATION

In Midland, cyclists favor the **Pere Marquette Rail-Trail** (989/832-6870), a 30-mile-long asphalt trail that's also a hit for those on foot, with in-line skates, or with wheelchairs or strollers. It begins in downtown Midland near the **Tridge,** a three-way pedestrian footbridge spanning the confluence of the Tittabawassee and Chippewa Rivers. The Tridge is a local landmark, and a gathering spot for picnics, concerts, festivals, and more. From there, the rail-trail follows Saginaw Road to Coleman, passing by the Dow Historical Museum and Bradley Home before reaching the towns of Averill and Sanford.

Hikers have another option in Midland. After a visit in the 1970s, the vice president of the National Audubon Society called the **Chippewa Nature Center** (400 S. Badour Rd., 989/631-0830, www.chippewanaturecenter.com, visitors center 8am-5pm Mon.-Fri., 9am-5pm Sat., 1pm-5pm Sun., free) "one of the finest—if not *the* finest—private nature centers in the world." More recently, the National Park Service cited the center for its outstanding educational accomplishments and designated it a National Environmental Study Area. The 1,200-acre center sits along the Pine River and was designed (not surprisingly) by Alden Dow to merge with the living world around it. Its most striking feature is the River Overlook, a 60-foot-long, glass-walled room cantilevered over the Pine River, with great views of the center's birdlife and wildlife.

The center offers an unusually rich mix of things to see, including an authentic log homestead, items discovered from on-site archaeological digs, and a display that's a good all-around introduction to the area's natural

the Tridge, a unique footbridge in Midland

the Chippewa Nature Center

history. Other highlights include well-executed dioramas that show Michigan geology and scenes from the Saginaw Valley Indian culture. Despite the wide range of attractions, the center's hallmark is the seclusion, peace, and beauty of its surroundings. A map available at the visitors center guides visitors through the 13-mile trail system that parallels the Chippewa River. Popular with hikers and cross-country skiers, the trails include artificially created wetlands, begun in 1990 to compensate for a wetlands destroyed to build a nearby shopping mall.

ACCOMMODATIONS AND FOOD

Although Midland is no mecca of lodging and dining options, you'll find a variety of dependable chain motels clustered near the intersection of Wackerly and Eastman. Try the 90-room **Fairview Inn** (2200 W. Wackerly St., 989/631-0070, www.fairviewinnmidland.com, $79-109 d).

Not far from the hotel is **Bamboo Garden** (721 S. Saginaw Rd., 989/832-7967, 11am-10pm Mon.-Sat., 1pm-7pm Sun., $9-16), a classy Chinese restaurant with a relaxing atmosphere and reliably good food, including sizzling steak, Buddha duck, and moo shu pork with Mandarin pancakes.

Camping

For campers, **Black Creek State Forest Campground** (220 W. Ellsworth, 989/275-5151, daily mid-Apr.-Nov., $20 daily) offers 23 semi-modern sites (as in no electricity or showers), which can accommodate tents or RVs. Sites are available on a first-come, first-served basis. Campers can enjoy nearby hiking trails, bird-watching opportunities, a boat launch, and access to several lakes and rivers ideal for anglers.

INFORMATION AND SERVICES

For more information about the Midland area, contact the **Midland County Convention & Visitors Bureau** (300 Rodd St., 989/839-9522, www.midlandcvb.org). For other services, you'll have no trouble finding groceries, banks, post offices, and the like. If you need help in an emergency situation, dial **911** from any cell or public phone. For medical assistance, head to the **MidMichigan Medical Center** (4005 Orchard Dr., 989/839-3000, www.midmichigan.org).

GETTING THERE AND AROUND

Travelers can fly directly into the **MBS International Airport** (MBS, 8500 Garfield Rd., Freeland, 989/695-5555, www.mbsairport.org), where it's possible to rent a car from one of five major rental agencies. From there, head to Midland via Garfield Road, US-10 West, and M-20 West; without traffic, the 13-mile trip should take about 20 minutes.

Of course, most folks will likely be driving from elsewhere in Michigan. From Mount Pleasant, for instance, you can simply take M-20 East to downtown Midland, a 27-mile trip that usually takes about 33 minutes. From downtown Bay City, meanwhile, you can just take M-25 West, continue onto US-10 West, and follow M-20 West to downtown Midland; without traffic, the 19-mile trip takes roughly 23 minutes. Once you've arrived, you can then drive, bike, or walk around town.

MAP SYMBOLS

▦▦▦	Expressway	◖	Highlight	✗	Airfield	⚓	Golf Course
⋯⋯	Primary Road	○	City/Town	✈	Airport	Ⓟ	Parking Area
▦▦▦	Secondary Road	◉	State Capital	▲	Mountain	⛰	Archaeological Site
⬚⬚⬚	Unpaved Road	⊛	National Capital	✦	Unique Natural Feature	⬛	Church
------	Trail	★	Point of Interest			🛢	Gas Station
⋯⋯⋯	Ferry	•	Accommodation	⋰	Waterfall	▦	Glacier
-·-·-·	Railroad	▾	Restaurant/Bar	▲	Park	▦	Mangrove
▦▦▦	Pedestrian Walkway	■	Other Location	⊟	Trailhead	▦	Reef
⬚⬚⬚	Stairs	⋀	Campground	⛷	Skiing Area	▦	Swamp

CONVERSION TABLES

°C = (°F - 32) / 1.8
°F = (°C x 1.8) + 32
1 inch = 2.54 centimeters (cm)
1 foot = 0.304 meters (m)
1 yard = 0.914 meters
1 mile = 1.6093 kilometers (km)
1 km = 0.6214 miles
1 fathom = 1.8288 m
1 chain = 20.1168 m
1 furlong = 201.168 m
1 acre = 0.4047 hectares
1 sq km = 100 hectares
1 sq mile = 2.59 square km
1 ounce = 28.35 grams
1 pound = 0.4536 kilograms
1 short ton = 0.90718 metric ton
1 short ton = 2,000 pounds
1 long ton = 1.016 metric tons
1 long ton = 2,240 pounds
1 metric ton = 1,000 kilograms
1 quart = 0.94635 liters
1 US gallon = 3.7854 liters
1 Imperial gallon = 4.5459 liters
1 nautical mile = 1.852 km

°FAHRENHEIT / °CELSIUS

°FAHRENHEIT	°CELSIUS	
230	110	
220		
210	100	WATER BOILS
200		
190	90	
180	80	
170		
160	70	
150		
140	60	
130	50	
120		
110	40	
100		
90	30	
80		
70	20	
60		
50	10	
40		
30	0	WATER FREEZES
20		
10	-10	
0		
-10	-20	
-20	-30	
-30		
-40	-40	

INCH: 0 1 2 3 4

CM: 0 1 2 3 4 5 6 7 8 9 10

MOON DETROIT & ANN ARBOR
Avalon Travel
a member of the Perseus Books Group
1700 Fourth Street
Berkeley, CA 94710, USA
www.moon.com

Editor: Erin Raber
Series Manager: Kathryn Ettinger
Copy Editor: Ann Seifert
Graphics Coordinator: Elizabeth Jang
Production Coordinator: Elizabeth Jang
Cover Designer: Kathryn Osgood
Map Editor: Kat Bennett
Cartographers: Kat Bennett, Stephanie Poulain

ISBN-13: 978-1-61238-788-8

KEEPING CURRENT

If you have a favorite gem you'd like to see included in the next edition, or see anything
that needs updating, clarification, or correction, please drop us a line. Send your com-
ments via email to feedback@moon.com, or use the address above.

ABOUT THE AUTHOR

Laura Martone

Laura Martone has been an avid traveler since childhood. While growing up, she and her mother would often take long road trips to fascinating U.S. landmarks, such as the Rocky Mountains and Monticello. After graduating from Northwestern University in 1998 with a dual degree in English and radio/TV/film, Laura continued to explore the United States with her husband, Daniel. Equally fond of cultural and natural wonders, she has a particular affinity for the state of Michigan, where she spends her summers.

Laura first traveled to the Great Lakes State in 2000 to visit her husband's family and has experienced a lot of this diverse locale ever since. She's searched for Petoskey stones along the shores of Lake Superior, picked wild blueberries in the woods of the Lower Peninsula, toured an active GM truck plant in the Flint area, explored the art galleries of Saugatuck and Douglas, and attended the National Cherry Festival in Traverse City – and she's not done yet.

When not in Michigan, Laura operates two film festivals with her husband and spends much of her time in New Orleans. She's contributed articles to *National Geographic Traveler, MotorHome, Route 66 Magazine, RV Journal,* and *The Ecotourism Observer.* In addition, she's written and edited several other guidebooks, including *Moon New Orleans, Moon Florida Keys, Moon Baja RV Camping,* and *Moon Metro Los Angeles.* For more about Laura's travels, visit her websites at www.wanderingsoles.com and www.americannomadtravel.com.

CPSIA information can be obtained at www.ICGtesting.com
Printed in the USA
LVOW10s1128100614

389391LV00005B/27/P